FISH

Richard Ellis

ABRAMS, NEW YORK

CONTENTS

PRECEDING SPREAD *Great white shark chasing California sea lions through a kelp forest.*

OPPOSITE *Except for man, the only creature capable of taking down a full-grown swordfish is a mako shark.*

Zane Grey, author of Western novels such as Riders of the Purple Sage, and conqueror of this Australian great white shark.

HOW BIG IS A BIG FISH?

IN THE OLD TESTAMENT, God orders Jonah to go to the city of Nineveh, in modern-day northern Iraq, to preach against wickedness. Jonah, seeking to avoid God's command, travels instead to Joppa, the Mediterranean port now known as Jaffa. There, he embarks on a ship heading for Tarshish, a name used in the Bible to connote a distant place, sometimes associated by scholars with Spain or Greece, and so Jonah is on the Mediterranean sailing west. When a great storm threatens to sink the ship, Jonah, understanding that he is the target of God's wrath, tells his fellow sailors that the waters will be calmed only if they toss him overboard. Here comes what is probably the first big fish in literature: "Now the Lord had prepared a great fish to swallow up Jonah. And Jonah was in the belly of the fish three days and three nights" (Jonah 1:17). From inside the fish, Jonah offers a prayer of repentance, and he is saved: "And the Lord spake unto the fish, and it vomited out Jonah upon the dry land" (Jonah 2:10).

According to popular tradition, the beast that swallowed Jonah was a whale. Now, there are whales in the Mediterranean, but the Bible specifically says "a great fish," and Genesis distinguishes between "the great whales" (Genesis 1:21) and "the fish of the sea" (Genesis 1:26). If one of the fish of the sea swallowed old Jonah, which one was it? There are some pretty big fish in the Mediterranean, including bluefin tuna (which can weigh more than half a ton), but tuna are not designed to swallow anything much larger than a mackerel, so we have to look elsewhere. In his *Life of Sharks* (1971), Paul Budker alludes to an intellectual tradition going back at least to the sixteenth-century French naturalist Guillaume Rondelet that identifies the fish that swallowed Jonah as a shark: "The impossibility of passing a man down the narrow throat of a whale led Rondelet to search for a marine animal capable of swallowing such a large prey and bringing it up whole later on. *Carcharodon carcharias*, the great white shark, was not a bad choice." (While the great white shark's anatomy might permit it to swallow a person whole, there are no known instances of one regurgitating a person alive—something to do with that great mouthful of razor-sharp teeth, perhaps—but never mind.)

We may never know exactly what kind of creature swallowed Jonah, but we can figure out what "a great fish" actually is. First, we have to define fish. According to the *Oxford English Dictionary* (*OED*), the term was originally applied to any animal living exclusively in water, such as *crayfish, cuttlefish, jellyfish,* or *shellfish.* We all know that a crayfish, a cuttlefish, or a jellyfish is not actually a *fish,* and, indeed, the term is now reserved for "any of a large and varied group of cold-blooded aquatic vertebrates possessing gills and fins." There are more than twenty-one thousand fish species, found in all the planet's wild waters, from freshwater lakes, rivers, and ponds to all the oceans: warm, cold, salty, tepid, ice-choked, deep, dark, rough, calm, shallow, and sunlit.

Most of the world's fish have a bony skeleton and are classified as osteichthyes (a literal rendering of "bony fish"); these fish are also known as teleosts, from the Greek *teleos,* which means "complete" and refers to the total ossification of the skeleton. There are also "fish" with no bones at all, but rather a skeleton composed exclusively of cartilage. (The same *OED* tells us that a skeleton is "the bones or bony framework of an animal body considered as a whole," so "cartilaginous skeleton" may be a bit of an oxymoron, but we can get around this contradiction by employing a secondary dictionary definition, "the harder [supporting or covering] constituent part of an animal organism." The hard [supporting] parts—the *exoskeleton*—of insects, spiders, gastropods, bivalves, crustaceans, and snails are on the outside, and of course there are no bones there, either.) The cartilaginous fish comprise the sharks and rays, also known as elasmobranchs

† In 1982, I traveled to the Azores in an attempt to track down this photograph, which would have been by far the longest great white on record. I interviewed whalers and fishermen, examined newspapers and photograph collections, and even offered a reward for any evidence of this monster. I found nothing to corroborate Wood's story. It turned out that the photo was actually of a sixteen-footer, that it had not been taken where or when he said it had, and that the photographer was not the person he said it was. Was it an outright fabrication? We will never know.

(derived from the Greek word for metal and the Latin word for gills and referring to their multiple gill slits), and the chimaeras. In these creatures everything but the teeth is made of cartilage. The sharks and rays developed more or less simultaneously with, and possibly later than, the bony fish, and are in no way more "primitive" than the osteichthyes.

Chimaeras are weird-looking deepwater creatures that usually do not exceed four feet in length (most are smaller), and while they are more than a little interesting, they will not concern us here. We are interested in the *big* fish, bony or cartilaginous. So was Australian ichthyologist David G. Stead, author of *Giants and Pigmies of the Deep: The Story of Australia's Sea Denizens* (1933). Many of Stead's denizens are not found exclusively in Australia's waters, so his little book can serve as a general introduction to extra-large sea creatures. Of course, a large proportion of Stead's "giants" are cetaceans (that is, whales), but he also discusses big sharks (mostly man-eaters, of course), billfish, tuna, giant groupers (known as "gropers" in Australia), sea bass, and ocean sunfish. His book concludes with an evaluation of sea-serpent sightings, many of which he believes to have been the "giant calamary" (squid) or various large eels. In another volume, Stead credulously incorporated a report of what would have been the largest fish ever sighted, a ghostly white shark that was "three hundred feet long at least," had anyone actually been able to measure it.

Five years after Stead's book, John Roxborough Norman, an ichthyologist at the Natural History Museum in London, and Sir Francis Fraser, a cetologist at the same institution, published *Giant Fishes, Whales, and Dolphins* (1938). The mammals known as dolphins will make only cameo appearances in this book, usually as supporting cast members in a story that involves multiple vertebrate species (think of the "tuna-porpoise problem," in which tuna fishermen once set their nets around aggregations of yellowfin or skipjack tuna, but hauled in thousands of dolphins as well), and whales will occasionally be used for size comparisons (as we will see, there are a couple of shark species that can get to be as large or larger than many whale species, and there is an extinct fish that reached the almost unimaginable length of one hundred feet, as big as a blue whale). Norman and Fraser did not bother much with definitions (or consistency); they included many of the larger sharks but among the bony

fish they threw in the very un-giant mackerel, remoras, and flying fish.

A book that, by definition, includes the biggest fish is Gerald Wood's *Guinness Book of Animal Facts and Feats* (1982). It encompasses the largest and fastest mammals, the largest and smallest birds, the largest and most dangerous insects, the deadliest snakes, the largest-known natural pearl, and so on, but there is also a detailed accounting of big fish, the subject of our current study. Of course this book includes the whale shark and the basking shark, the great white shark, and the ocean sunfish (Wood reproduces a photograph of a *Mola mola* said to weigh 4,928 pounds, which he calls "the largest of the bony fishes"; it is certainly the heaviest). There are photographs of giant Mekong catfish and the European catfish, or wels, and an illustration of a man sitting on an arapaima that looks as if it weighed at least eight hundred pounds. The book also contains a description of a 37-foot-long great white shark and a photograph of what is identified as a 29.6-footer "harpooned by Azorean fishermen in 1978."† As with many Guinness "records," at least a few of these facts and feats appear to have been enhanced—or even fabricated—to qualify them for inclusion.

There are thousands of books about fish, ranging from the technical to the popular, and many that concentrate on a particular species, but these are among the few that categorize fish by size. Francesca LaMonte, a former associate curator of fish at the American Museum of Natural History in New York, was particularly interested in game fish and fishing; she is probably best known for her handbooks *North American Game Fishes* (1945) and *Marine Game Fishes of the World* (1952). Dearest to our hearts here, however, is her *Giant Fishes of the Open Sea* (1965), a large-format children's book that recounts LaMonte's experiences with tuna, swordfish, sharks, and marlins. When Australian angler Peter Goadby wanted to write about game fishing in the Pacific, he titled his book *Big Fish and Blue Water* (1970), primarily because of the massive size of the world's premier saltwater game fish, the marlins, tuna, and swordfish. Goadby's book contains capsule description of game fish found in his local waters, and it also provides angling tips, along with plentiful advice about boats, clothing, camera equipment, food, drink, and seasickness.

Before I embark on my own survey of the big fish, roughly defined here as species that grow to be substantially larger and

heavier than the largest human being—but also, I confess, a list of my personal favorites—I need to say a word about bony versus cartilaginous fish, in regard to size. Although some of the "big fish," such as the tuna and billfish, have bony skeletons, a surprising number of very large ocean dwellers are sharks or rays. (As with the sharks, most rays are smallish and not particularly intimidating, but the giant sawfish and the giant manta, both of which are harmless to people, were long considered frightening sea monsters thanks to their impressive sizes.) In addition, two of the largest fish alive today, the giant sturgeon and the Chinese paddlefish, are classed with the teleosts but are largely cartilaginous. (Maybe not "alive today"—the Chinese paddlefish [see pages 122–3] is, as of 2007, believed to be extinct.)

In today's oceans, the largest sharks—the whale shark, basking shark, Greenland shark, and great white shark—are considerably larger than the largest of the bony fish, the marlins, tuna, and swordfish. This cannot be a function of bone versus cartilage alone, for the largest creatures in the ocean—indeed, the largest creatures that have ever lived on earth—have bony

skeletons. I speak of the whales, of course, seagoing mammals that exceed in length and weight any fish or shark. The great blue whale, at a known length of one hundred feet and a weight of 150 tons, far surpasses the size of any fish or shark, but also the size of any known dinosaur, such as the gigantic "supersaurus," now recognized to be the largest known plant-eating dinosaur. (As far as we know, carnivorous dinosaurs such as the *Tyrannosaurus rex* never approached this size, reaching an estimated forty feet in length, while some of the early carnivorous marine reptiles, such as *Kronosaurus* or *Liopleurodon*, may have been fifty feet long.) In addition to the blue whale, the fin, sei, bowhead, and right whales all exceed the maximum length and weight of the great sharks, evidence that bony skeletons can provide the framework for gigantism in the ocean. So we must look elsewhere for an explanation of why today's cartilaginous fishes so dominate the record books.

Along with the great baleen whales, the whale shark and the basking shark are filter feeders rather than predators, swimming slowly through schools of tiny animals and trapping them in a sievelike arrangement in their mouths before swallowing them. It is almost possible, then, to correlate great size in sea animals with filter feeding. As if to support such a correlation, we see that one of the largest marine predators, the fifty-foot-long, fifteen-ton shark Megalodon, is now extinct. As with so many extinctions, we cannot identify the actual "reason" that Megalodon disappeared; but its prey—mostly large, ancestral whales—lives on in the form of today's whales, so it did not die off because it ran out of things to eat. Its demise may have had something to do with a seismic rearrangement of the world's ocean basins, a global temperature change, an impact from space, or something that has not occurred to us yet, but whatever it was, Megalodon is no longer with us.

On land and in the sea, the giant predators are gone, victims of some aspect of the extinction scenario that we cannot explain, except to say that they are not here any more. (The only holdover is the sperm whale, a sixty-foot-long, sixty-ton toothed leviathan that feeds on squid in the depths of the oceans.) The largest extant carnivorous shark is the great white, only a third of the length and heft of Megalodon. Of course, these extinct predators are not alone. Almost everything that has ever lived on earth has become extinct. It has been estimated that 99.9 percent of all species that

have ever existed are gone. Although we are (rightly) concerned nowadays with anthropogenic, or human-caused, extinctions, it is a fact of life that every species, no matter how numerous, big, aggressive, clever, or dominant, will eventually disappear. That goes for you and yours, too.

The giants will always topple, but in recent times, the big fish have been chased, captured, and, more often than not, eaten to the brink of extinction by human beings. Of course, there is more to eat on a big fish than on a smaller one, so hunting the giants has a certain practical aspect. Villagers in Amazonia caught and ate the giant arapaima; along the Mekong River in Southeast Asia, a single giant catfish could provide food for a small village; and giant sturgeon, edible enough on their own, once provided the most valuable eggs in the world—for which the fish had to die. For thousands of years, Mediterranean fishermen trapped bluefin tuna in offshore net complexes, feeding ancient Spanish, Italian, and Sicilian villagers. There is plenty of meat on a half-ton swordfish or a bluefin tuna that weighs five hundred pounds more than that, but it has only been within the past century and a half, with the development of industrial fishing, that these giants of the western North Atlantic could be caught in commercially viable numbers. Prior to the introduction of longlines, commercial rigs carrying hundreds or thousands of baited hooks, tuna and swordfish were harpooned one at a time—sort of like whales, only the fish had gills and vertical tails.

Some of the big fish you will meet in this book have an inner structure of bone where others have cartilage. Some live near the surface; others inhabit the abyssal depths. Some live in deep offshore waters, others live in lakes or rivers close to human habitation. Some are regarded as dangerous "man-eaters," while others are harmless to anything but their normal prey. Some put up a gallant, acrobatic fight when hooked; others sink like stubborn, submerged boulders. For all their variety, however, there is one thing that can be said with absolute certainty about all the big fish: Their length, weight, and fighting ability will almost always be exaggerated when reported by human observers.

Left to right: Richard Ellis (partially hidden), Peter Benchley, and Captain Frank Mundus ready to board the Cricket II *for a day of shark fishing out of Montauk, Long Island.*

Zane Grey demonstrating the rig he used for big-game fishing.

The temptation to magnify the sizes of big fish is endemic; videlicet that paradigm for gross exaggeration, the "fish story."

Zane Grey, famous for fictionalizing the American West in novels such as *Riders of the Purple Sage* (1912) also wrote several books about his fishing exploits. His *Tales of Swordfish and Tuna* (1927) recounted his adventures in fighting and landing these giants. Ernest Hemingway also wrote about big fish—in *The Old Man and the Sea* (1952) and *Islands in the Stream* (1970)—but in my opinion, the best teller of big-fish stories was Peter Benchley. He wrote about giant sharks (*Jaws*, 1974), giant manta rays (*The Girl of the Sea of Cortez*, 1983), and giant squid (*Beast*, 1991), and while he may have exaggerated the size and the motivation of certain subjects, I know that within (or without) the confines of the novel, he tried to get the biology right. If he did not always succeed, I think we can attribute that "failure" to the demands of commercial storytelling, and he was very, very good at that. Toward the end of his life—he died in 2006—Benchley devoted himself to correcting the erroneous impression that sharks were evil and ought to be killed however and wherever possible. In an article in *Audubon* magazine in 1998, he wrote, "I couldn't possibly write *Jaws* today. We know so much more about sharks—and just as important, about our position as the single most careless, voracious, carnivorous destroyer of life on earth—that the notion of demonizing a fish strikes me as insane." He was right. This book is for my friend Peter Benchley.

BLUEFIN TUNA, 12'
see page 103

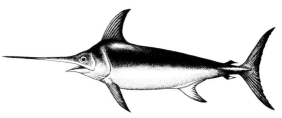

SWORDFISH, 15'
see page 89

SELECTED FISH & THEIR
RELATIVE SIZES

SCALE: one foot = 5 millimeters

ARAPAIMA, 10'
see page 127

WHALE SHARK, 50'
see page 26

XIPHACTINUS, 20'
see page 23

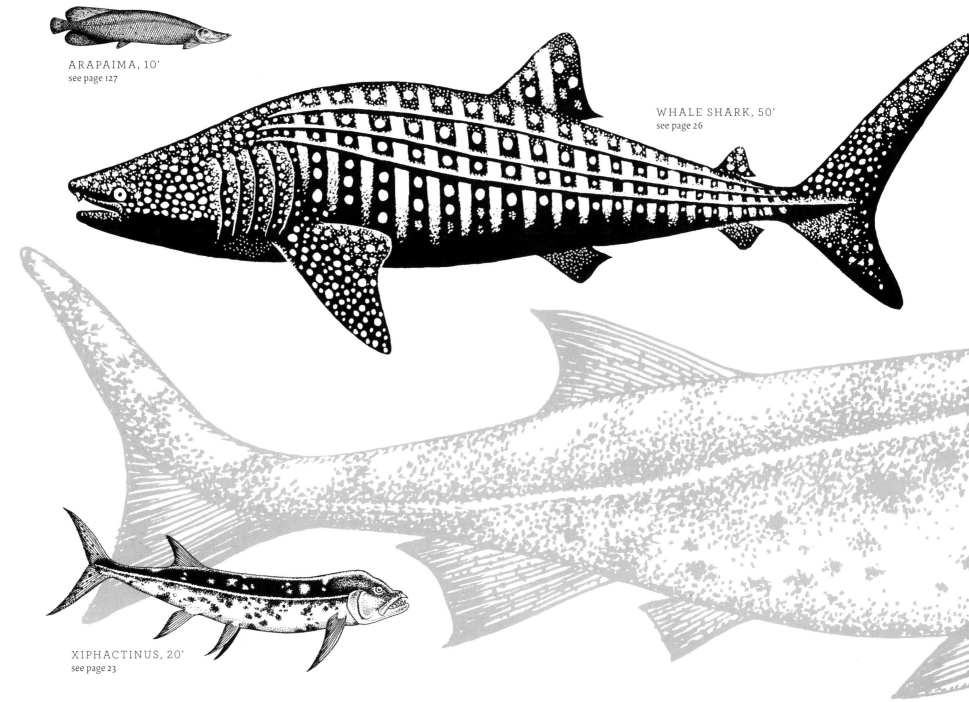

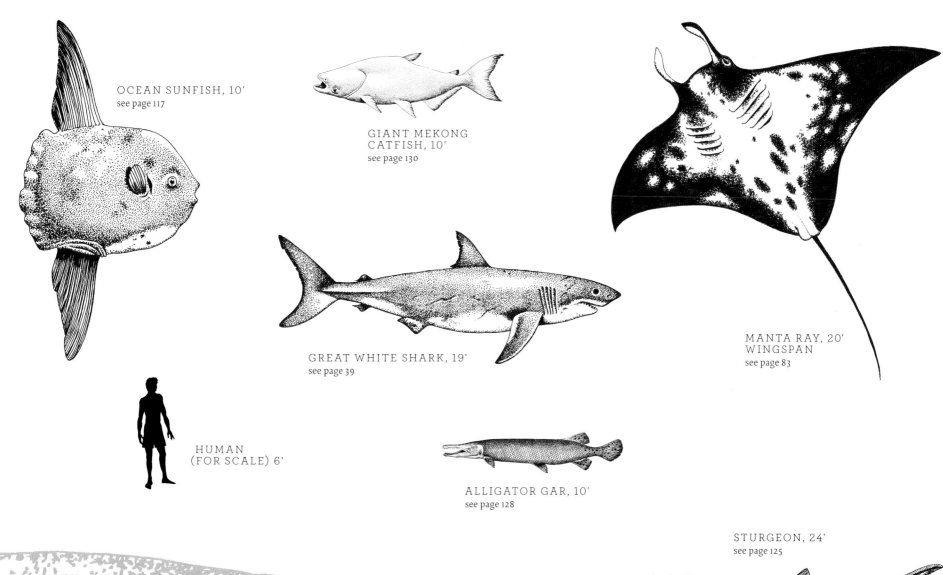

OCEAN SUNFISH, 10'
see page 117

GIANT MEKONG
CATFISH, 10'
see page 130

MANTA RAY, 20'
WINGSPAN
see page 83

GREAT WHITE SHARK, 19'
see page 39

HUMAN
(FOR SCALE) 6'

ALLIGATOR GAR, 10'
see page 128

STURGEON, 24'
see page 125

LEEDSICHTHYS, 80'
see page 19

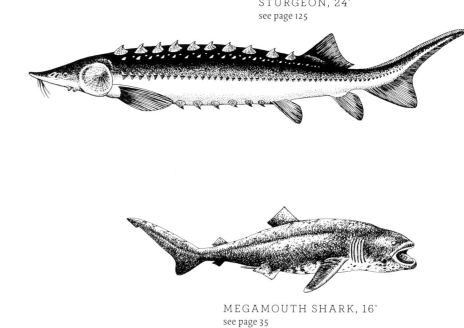

MEGAMOUTH SHARK, 16'
see page 35

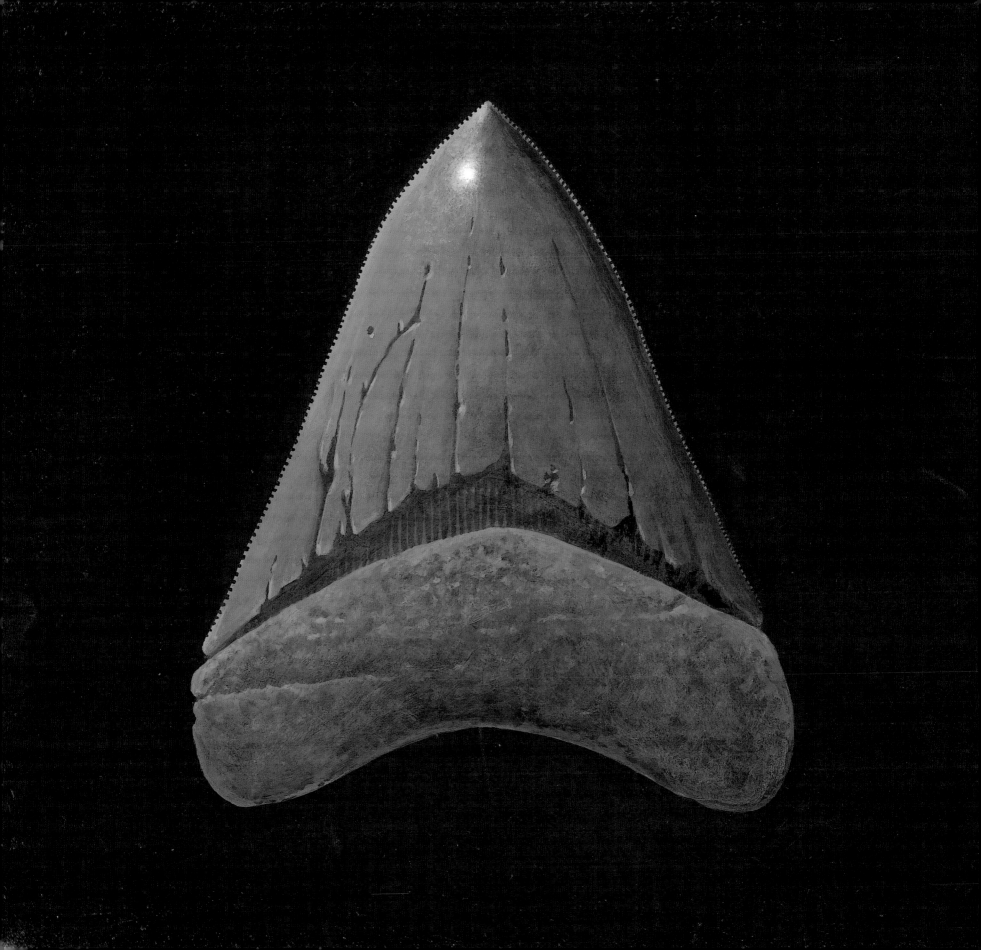

BIG FISH IN THE DISTANT PAST

DUNKLEOSTEUS

LEEDSICHTHYS

MEGALODON

XIPHACTINUS

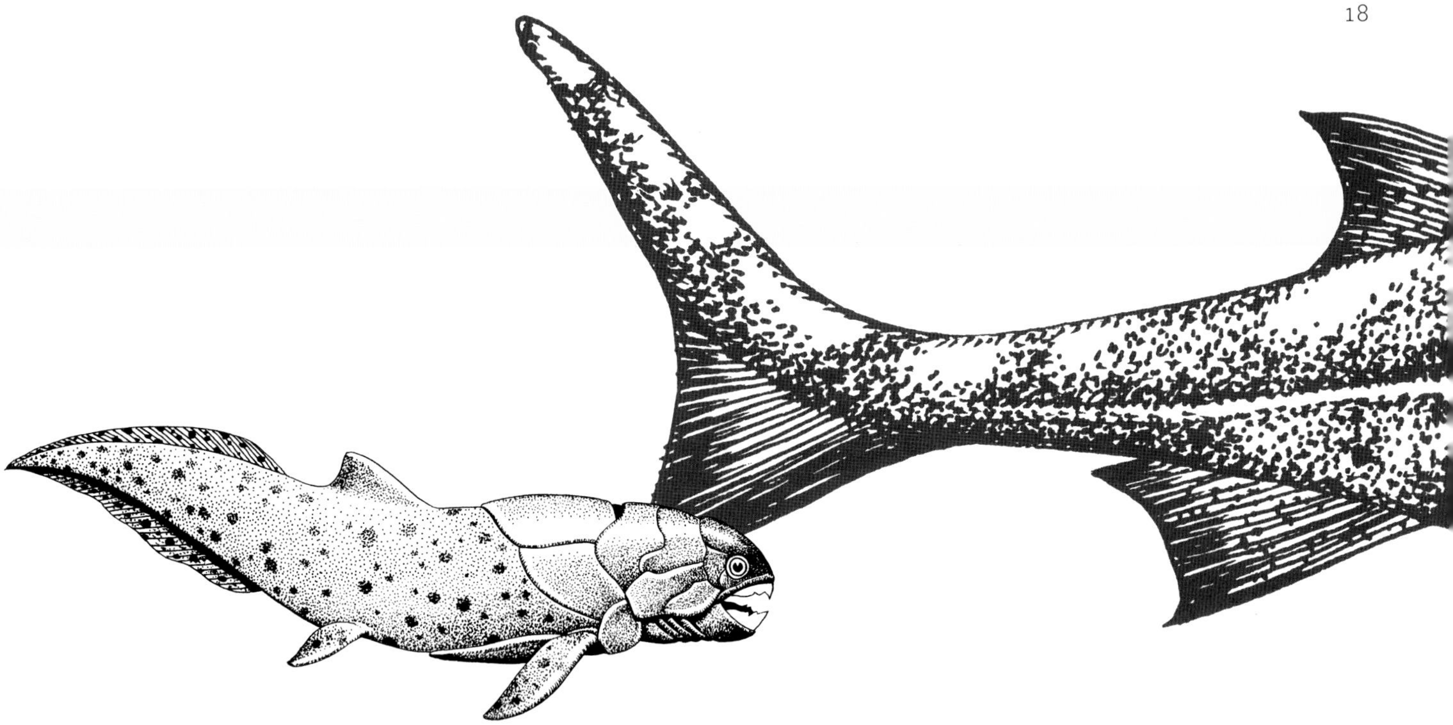

DUNKLEOSTEUS

ABOVE *We ought to be thankful that the 30-foot-long Dunkleosteus has been extinct for 450 million years.*

PREVIOUS *A fossilized tooth of Megalodon, shown actual size. If anyone ever found a white Megalodon tooth, it would indicate that this fifty-foot monster still roams the seas.*

THE FIRST "FISH"—VERTEBRATES that extracted oxygen from water by means of gills—were agnathans, meaning they had no jaws. (Agnathans is from the Greek *a* meaning "without" plus *gnathos* meaning "jaw.") They are among the oldest vertebrates, some dating from 450 million years ago. From the fossil record, we know that many were heavily armored, but some were eel-like in form, like the living agnathans, the lampreys and hagfish.

The first jawed fish, the gnathostomes, were characterized by head-and-shoulder girdles that were heavily armored with bony plates. Appearing first in the early Devonian period (between 360 and 415 million years ago), the placoderms (Greek for "plate-skins") were a diverse group of early gnathostomes that included thirty-five families and more than 270 genera. There are no placoderms known after the early Carboniferous period (350 million years ago), and no living fish show any of the characteristics of these primitive creatures. The largest placoderm was the formidable *Dunkleosteus*, which may have reached a length of thirty feet. Although its foreparts were encased in heavy armor, its long, eel-like tail could propel it powerfully through the water. There used to be another armored fish of equivalent size known as *Dinichthys*. That is, "used to be" in a taxonomic sense; with the same characteristics as *Dunklosteus*, the two species may actually be the same. These armored beasts are known as dinichthids (from the Greek *dino*, meaning "terrible" or "fearful," the same root that gave us *dinosaurs*, the "terrible lizards," and *ichthus*, or "fish").

A thirty-foot-long, armor-plated monster with jaws like a gigantic staple remover, *Dunkleosteus* was arguably the first big fish and also the first apex predator. Other inhabitants of the Devonian oceans were no match for *Dunkleosteus*, which would have been able to catch any primitive shark or fish (many of which were also armor plated) and chomp them into swallowable pieces with its bladelike fangs. Phillip Anderson and Mark Westneat of the Field Museum in Chicago built a model of the jaws of *Dunkleosteus* to see how they actually worked and concluded that this giant fish had "one of the most powerful bites in vertebrate history," equaled (maybe) by today's larger crocodiles and the great carnivorous dinosaurs. They were able to demonstrate that the predator's jaws, articulated by a unique mechanism based on four rotational joints working in harmony, snapped shut with a force of more than five tons. This monster fish cruised the oceans, preying on creatures much larger than itself. One of the most fearsome predators that ever lived, *Dunkleosteus* predated the carnivorous dinosaurs by a couple of hundred million years and the carnivorous marine reptiles, such as *Liopleurodon*, by about a hundred million.

LEEDSICHTHYS

THE PACHYCORMIDS WERE BONY FISH of the Early Jurassic period (between 175 and 205 million years ago) that were characterized by a streamlined body shape, pointed snout, scythelike pectorals, a narrow caudal peduncle (or tail stock, the end of the body to which the tail is attached), and a deeply forked tail. In other words, they were shaped not unlike today's sharks. Most of them, like *Pachycormus*, were about four feet long, but *Leedsichthys* was probably the largest fish that ever lived. Fossils found in the London Clay Formation of Britain suggest that *Leedsichthys problematicus* reached a length of forty feet, but there have been published estimates of specimens twice that long. Its tail—which constitutes the best-preserved fossil evidence of its existence—measured some sixteen feet from tip to tip. In *Fossils of the Oxford Clay* (1991), David Martill describes it as "a fish of gigantic proportions.... Skull bones massive, irregular, and often difficult to identify.... Ribs massive." "*Leedsichthys*," wrote Michael Benton in *Vertebrate Paleontology* (1990), "was a monstrous scaleless filter feeder up to 10m [33 feet] in length."

Leedsichthys would have dwarfed every other animal in the sea, but it was a gentle giant that lived on the tiny shrimps,

ABOVE *At a length approaching 100 feet,* Leedsichthys *is probably the largest fish that ever lived.*

jellyfish, and small fish that make up plankton. It would have swum slowly through the ocean's upper waters, taking mouthfuls of plankton-rich water and sieving them through giant mesh plates at the back of its mouth. Its feeding habits were similar to the modern blue whale, which also survives on nothing but plankton. This great fish probably traveled large distances to find parts of the world where seasonal conditions caused plankton to form itself into a dense, concentrated organic soup. Once a year, and probably after plankton feasts, *Leedsichthys* would have shed the giant filter plates from the back of its mouth, rendering it unable to feed itself for several weeks while the new ones grew back. Toward the end of this time it would have become weakened through hunger and vulnerable to attack. The Jurassic seas in which *Leedsichthys* lived were dangerous, and despite its size, it would have had no means of defending itself against predators such as the pliosaurs or the mosasaurs, giant seagoing reptiles. One attack would have been unlikely to kill a full-grown *Leedsichthys*, but several predators could have inflicted fatal damage, leaving the defenseless giant to die slowly as its attackers fed on the living carcass.

Because we have very scant fossil evidence, we really have no idea what *Leedsichthys* actually looked like. From the preserved tail, however, we know it was an actinopterygian, or a ray-finned fish, as are the great majority of living fish today. These fish are called "ray-finned" because their fins consist of webs of skin reinforced by bony spines. With numerous variations, today's actinopterygians have large gill-covers (opercula) and a suite of fins that usually consists of one (or occasionally more) dorsal fins, two pectoral fins, one or two pelvic fins, an anal fin, and a caudal (or tail) fin. In the more than twenty thousand living fish species there are any number of variations on this theme: Codfish, for instance, have three dorsal fins; tails come in all configurations from paddle shaped to crescent moon to eel-like trailer; and the fast-swimming scombrids (tuna, marlins, mackerel) have a series of "finlets" just forward of the tail. Most bony fish sport the traditional fin arrangement and so do most sharks, but sharks have multiple gill openings. I have therefore drawn *Leedsichthys* as if it were some kind of a bigmouthed herring (with basking shark overtones). Keep in mind that this drawing is almost wholly conjectural, and nothing about it represents the (very limited) state of our knowledge of this enigmatic giant.

MEGALODON

Put in only for scale, neither the great white shark nor the human diver existed at the same time as Megalodon.

IF THE WHITE SHARK, AT TWENTY FEET LONG and with a mouth big enough to swallow a small child, is not terrifying enough, try to imagine a creature that is three times as long, probably four times as heavy, and with a mouth large enough to swallow a cow. This is the stuff of nightmares. Monster lovers will be delighted to learn that this creature actually existed, but those who swim in the world's oceans will be grateful to know that it no longer exists. The giant shark, which most paleontologists believe became extinct about one hundred thousand years ago, was called *Carcharodon megalodon*; *Carcharodon* because it is believed to be a close relative of the white shark (*Carcharodon carcharias*), and *megalodon*, meaning "big tooth." How big was it? The largest white shark tooth is a little more than two inches high, measured along its diagonal serrated edge. The longest known Megalodon tooth—a heavy, stonelike fossil—is almost eight inches long, approximately the size of a grown man's hand.

After dinosaur bones (and maybe trilobites), the teeth of this huge extinct shark, our primary souvenirs of its existence, are probably the most popular of all fossils. These teeth—always fossilized, despite some claims to the contrary—are heavy and triangular, with serrations along the blade. As they are shaped very much like those of today's great white shark, the star of *Jaws* and other Hollywood movies, so Megalodon comes to us with its reputation already in place. Abundant fossil evidence shows that Megalodon lived during the Middle and Late Tertiary periods, beginning fifty million years ago and ending in the relatively recent past, and probably wandered the same seas as the modern white shark, plying pretty much the same

trade—but on a substantially larger scale. In 1909, when a gigantic Megalodon jaw was placed on exhibit in the American Museum of Natural History in New York, curator Bashford Dean wrote, "At the entrance of the Hall of Fossil Fishes, there is now exhibited a restoration of the jaws of a shark (*Carcharodon megalodon*), which lived along the coast of South Carolina in Tertiary time. There can be no doubt that this was the largest and most formidable fish living or extinct of which we have any record. The jaws of a fully grown specimen measured about nine feet across and must have had a gape of five or six feet."

While Megalodon teeth closely resemble those of its smaller, living relative, the great white shark, the differences are sufficient to justify separating the extinct and recent sharks into distinct species: Besides their obviously greater size, Megalodon teeth have more and relatively smaller serrations and, above the root, a scar or "chevron" that is lacking on the teeth of adult *C. carcharias*.

Megalodon probably reached a length of around fifty feet, but everywhere there are those who want to increase its length. In a 1964 discussion of fossil teeth found at Uloa, South Africa, David Davies, director of the Oceanographic Research Institute in Durban, South Africa, wrote, "Estimates of size made from the fossil teeth of this wide-ranging shark obtained in various parts of the world indicate that it may have reached 60 to 80 feet in total length." People seem more than a little reluctant to concede the disappearance of some "prehistoric" animals (think of the "plesiosaur" of Loch Ness), and of these, the one that surfaces most regularly is the giant shark; not in the silly novels that play on the success of the *Jaws* phenomenon ("if they made all that money with a twenty-five-foot-long shark, think of what we could do with a hundred-footer"), but rather in works that might be taken seriously. In the section of David Stead's previously mentioned *Giants and Pigmies of the Deep* devoted to the white pointer shark, he wrote of Megalodon: "It reaches at least 40 feet, as far as observed specimens have been recorded, but teeth of a similar kind have been seen by me, which must have come from a specimen not less than 80 feet in length. Such a sea devil as this could comfortably accommodate one hundred humans at one meal!" Zane Grey firmly agreed that such monsters exist, and he cited Stead's account to prove it: "Dr. David Stead, of Sydney, a scientist of international reputation, corroborates my claim that there are white sharks up to eighty feet and more. If there are not, where do the shark teeth, five inches across the base, come from?... The waters around Australia are alive with many species of sharks. Why not some unknown species, huge and terrible? Who can tell what forms of life swim and battle in the ocean depths?"

The best-known report of living Megalodons from Stead's pen appeared in 1963, in a volume edited after his death by Gilbert P. Whitley:

> In the year 1918 I recorded the sensation that had been caused among the "outside" crayfishmen at Port Stephens, when, for several days, they refused to go to sea to their regular fishing grounds in the vicinity of Broughton Island. The men had been at work on the fishing grounds–which lie in deep water–when an immense shark of almost unbelievable proportions put in an appearance, lifting pot after pot containing many crayfishes, and taking, as the men said, "pots, mooring lines and all." These crayfish pots, it should be mentioned, were about 3-feet 6-inches in diameter and frequently contained from two to three dozen good-sized crayfish each weighing several pounds. The men were all unanimous that this shark was something the like of which they had never dreamed of. In company with the local Fisheries Inspector, I questioned many of the men very closely and they all agreed as to the gigantic stature of the beast. But the lengths they gave were, on the whole, absurd. I mention them, however, as an indication of the state of mind which this unusual giant had thrown them into. And bear in mind that these were men who were used to the sea and all sorts of weather, and all sorts of sharks as well. One of the crew said the shark was "three hundred feet long at least"! Others said it was as long as the

> wharf on which we stood–about 115 feet! They affirmed that the water "boiled" over a large space when the fish swam past. They were all familiar with whales, which they had often seen passing at sea, but this was a vast shark. They had seen its terrible head which was "at least as long as the roof of the wharf shed at Nelson's Bay." Impossible, of course! But these were prosaic and rather stolid men, not given to "fish stories" nor even to talking at all about their catches. Further, they knew that the person they were talking to (myself) had heard all the fish stories years before! One of the things that impressed me was that they all agreed as to the ghostly whitish color of the vast fish.

However, it is in the very abundance of fossilized Megalodon teeth that we find evidence that this giant shark is extinct. Sharks of all species have multiple rows of teeth; those currently doing the biting are replaced regularly in a process that has been likened to the action of a moving escalator. Behind the functional front rows of teeth there are other rows, waiting to move forward as those in the front rank fall out or are otherwise dislodged. A shark will therefore have many more teeth in its mouth during its lifetime than would any other vertebrate, the total number from a given animal across a lifetime numbering perhaps in the thousands. One might then suppose that it would not have required many individual Megalodons to have scattered all the teeth ever collected, but not so: We can be certain that hundreds of thousands or even millions more teeth remain on the seafloors or in the ground, most of them never to be seen. Despite the thousands of Megalodon teeth that have been dredged from the ocean floor or found embedded in the chalky cliffs of California, Maryland, Florida, North Carolina, Belgium, and Morocco, *not a single white one has ever been found.* All the teeth that have been unearthed or dredged up are brown or black, but the fact that they are not white does not mean they are not bone. A fossil bone is still bone, but one that sometimes contains a hard and heavy infilling of other minerals as well; the "bones" of the dinosaurs in various museums are no longer bone, but rather composed of compacted minerals that have gradually replaced the inorganic material (apatite) in the bones over time. Should someone, then, dredge up a *white* Megalodon tooth, we would know that the giant shark became extinct quite recently–or is flourishing somewhere in the vastness of the oceans and has simply lost a tooth.

XIPHACTINUS

PRONOUNCED "ZIFF-AC-TINIS" and sometimes known as the "bulldog fish," this denizen of the North American Cretaceous seas lived between sixty-five and ninety-five million years ago. It is classified as an ichthyodectid or "biting fish" (the Greek *dektos* means "bite"). Approximately the shape of a tarpon, Xiphactinus reached a known length of twenty feet—and may have gotten even larger. (There is no basis for the assumption that the fossils we find are the largest specimens; it is more than likely that we have not unearthed the largest ones.) With premaxillary fangs protruding from a mouth filled with nasty teeth, it was probably the dominant predator of the warm, shallow seas that covered much of the interior of modern-day North America in the Cretaceous period. On display at the Sternberg Museum of Natural History in Hays, Kansas, is a twelve-foot fossil of Xiphactinus with the complete skeleton of the smaller ichthyodectid *Gillicus* inside it. It would appear that the bulldog fish swallowed its prey whole, since other fossils of this species have also been found with undigested fish inside.

Xiphactinus, the bulldog fish, lived between 65 million and 95 million years ago. The color pattern is conjectural.

BIG SHARKS & RAYS

Whale Shark

Basking Shark

Megamouth Shark

Great White Shark

Mako Shark

Thresher Shark

Tiger Shark

Oceanic Whitetip Shark

Blue Shark

Bull Shark

Grey Nurse or
   Sand Tiger Shark

Hammerhead Shark

Goblin Shark

Sixgill Shark

Greenland Shark

Manta Ray

Sawfish

WHALE SHARK

PREVIOUS SPREAD *Portrait of* Carcharodon carcharias, *the star of four Hollywood movies.*

† Indeed, it is unmatched among any other whale sharks. Brad Norman, an Australian marine conservationist, recently established a photo-identification that showed that each whale shark has an individual pattern of stripes and spots. Based on a pattern-recognition method originally invented to study constellations in the night sky, the system will soon enable scores of coastal communities and thousands of individual divers to gather information about this gentle giant.

‡ In September 2007, Ecuadorean photographer Antonio Moreano photographed an all-white whale shark off Darwin Island in the Galápagos. Even though we know that it is a fish, it brings to mind nothing less than Moby Dick. See http://wetpixel.com/ i.php/full/albino-whale-shark-photographed-in-ecuador/

THE LARGEST FISH IN THE WORLD has a name that is guaranteed to confuse anyone but the experienced ichthyologist. It is called the whale shark, which is something like calling an animal a "cat-dog," or a "bird-snake." It sounds as if it might be either a whale or a shark, but we are not really sure which. It is, however, no relation whatever to the whales, which of course are mammals: *Rhincodon typus* (to eliminate the confusion, at least for the moment, by using its scientific name) is a cartilaginous fish. It has gills, breathes water, and does not come up for air. It is a shark, which means that in addition to the above characteristics, it has gill slits, a multitude of teeth, skin that is composed of dermal denticles, and a cartilaginous skeleton. The "whale" portion of its common name is simply a reference to its size.

The whale shark, however, is unique among the sharks, unique among the fish, and even unique among the vertebrates that inhabit the sea. First of all, it is gigantic when fully matured. We are not sure how big it can get; suffice it to say for now that it is a very big fish indeed, bigger than any other fish that swims. It is one of the few sharks whose mouth is in the "terminal" position, meaning that it is located at the front of the head rather than being underslung, as is the case with most other species of sharks. It might be assumed that the largest fish in the world would have little need of camouflage; in fact, it is almost impossible to imagine this behemoth hidden at all, especially since it inhabits the open ocean, where no plants grow. And yet the whale shark is covered in an intricate pattern of dots and stripes arranged in a very regular grid—a pattern that is unmatched anywhere else in nature.†

Starting at the broad head, the great fish is covered with a closely spaced pattern of dots, usually yellowish or white on a darker background. (The whale shark has been described as varying from dark gray to reddish or greenish brown on the back and sides, but most observers content themselves with a simple "brown" or "brownish.") From the snout to the pectorals, the dots are small and close together, but random in their placement. Above the pectorals, a more organized arrangement begins to appear, consisting of vertical rows of large dots (two to three inches in diameter), separated by vertical stripes. There are also strong horizontal ridges, which heighten the grid or checkerboard effect. The whale shark is lighter below, as are most sharks, and the tail is also spotted, but less densely than the foreparts.‡

Finally, the whale shark does not have the caudal notch that appears in every other large selachian. This peculiar "cut," located near the top of the trailing edge of the upper lobe of the tail fin, is visible on the tails of almost all other sharks, and no one seems to have the slightest idea of its purpose or function, if indeed it has one. It is probably unnecessary to assign a clear use to every lump, bump, and notch, but it seems unlikely that millions of years of evolution would have retained unnecessary structures. It is likely that there is (or was) a reason for this notch in the tail fin, but whatever it is, the whale shark does not seem to need it to survive.

In its external appearance then, *Rhincodon typus* (*Rhincodon* means "rasp tooth" or even "shark tooth"; it is the sole genus in the family Rhincodontidae) is nothing if not surprising. One's first impression is usually disbelief—is anything really this big? Add to this the bizarre markings and you end up thinking that no such creature can possibly exist.

Whale sharks are usually rare and solitary animals, although there have been instances in which more than one has been seen at a time—and even some occasions when small schools have been sighted. They are slow-moving, inquisitive creatures, and they have a tendency to hang around boats and divers, making no effort whatsoever to get away. American ichthyologist Dr. E. W.

PREVIOUS PAGE Portrait of a Lady with a Large Fish. *Sydney Gould (now Sydney Shuman) swims with a whale shark off Bermuda.*

RIGHT *A diver is dwarfed by a whale shark, the largest of all living fish.*

Gudger, of New York's American Museum of Natural History, had an ongoing preoccupation with whale sharks and tracked down every report, rumor, or suggestion of their occurrence, resulting in the publication of dozens of papers before World War II with titles such as "The Whale Shark in the Gulf of California," "The Food and Feeding Habits of the Whale Shark," and "The Whale Shark Unafraid." It was Gudger who obtained the seventeen-foot, four-inch specimen that was exhibited in 1931 in the Hall of Fishes at the museum; refurbished and repainted, it hangs there still.

Many of Gudger's accounts had to do with a whale shark being rammed by a ship ("Whale Sharks Rammed by Ocean Vessels"). This does not seem to be a particularly uncommon occurrence. The great fish seems unwilling to get out of the way of anything, and this recalcitrance often results in damage to the shark, the ship, or both. There have been accidents of this sort on a more or less regular basis since the largest fish in the world was discovered off the coast of South Africa in 1828. Given that this huge animal was unknown to science until the first quarter of the nineteenth century and possesses a habit of getting in the way of ships on the open sea, surely many sea-monster stories must have originated in encounters with whale sharks. As recently as 1905, when the liner *Armadale Castle* (J. C. Robinson, captain) collided with a "large fish," the creature was so poorly known that it could not be identified by any observer on the scene. An illustration published in a contemporaneous account, however, clearly shows that the large fish was a whale shark, complete with spots, ridges, and an unnotched tail. The size is given at "not less than 57 feet in length."

This brings us to the interesting question of the maximum size of *R. typus.* A careful search of the literature reveals many references to specimens of thirty-two to thirty-eight feet in length and a great deal of speculation about how big they might get. In Baja California waters, naturalist William Beebe saw a forty-two-footer from a boat and harpooned it, but could not bring it in. Again off Baja, Conrad Limbaugh of the Scripps Institution of Oceanography reported diving with a specimen "estimated to be 35–42 feet long." Bernard Heuvelmans's *In the Wake of Sea-Serpents* (1968) refers to several giant specimens, such as one, "53 feet long that was measured at Kommetje Bay in South Africa, and… even some 60 to 65 feet long, like the one which was caught in a bamboo fish-trap at Koh Chik in the east of the Gulf of Siam in 1919 but could not be measured accurately by a qualified person." These are the only references I have ever seen to these specimens, and without some corroboration, I am little inclined to accept them as fact.

In 1955, J. L. Baughman published a paper describing an event that shook the shark world. "Dredged up 130 miles south of Port Isabel, Texas, was a leathery egg case, the likes of which had never been seen before. It looked very much like the egg cases of other sharks and rays, but it measured twenty-seven by sixteen inches! Odell Freeze, a shrimp trawler who had found the case in one of his nets, 'felt something alive and kicking inside.' He carefully cut open the case and revealed a perfectly formed whale shark embryo, 14.5 inches long and complete with wide snout, stripes, spots, and lateral ridges." On the basis of this egg case, it was determined that whale sharks laid eggs, but in 1995, a female, measuring thirty-six feet, was harpooned off Taiwan (a known birthing area for the species) and three hundred fetal specimens were found in the two uteruses. It is now known that they are ovoviviparous, with the eggs hatching inside the uterus and the young being born alive. Freeze's discovery remains a mystery.

Whale sharks are found in all the tropical waters of the world. As with many tropical species, an occasional stray wanders into colder waters. The northernmost record is in the Bay of Fundy in Canada, and the southern limit seems to be South Africa, where the first whale shark ever seen by science was harpooned off Table Bay in 1828, far south of its usual range. They are not common anywhere, although this apparent rarity may be more a function of their deepwater existence than their possibly low population. A whale shark at the surface is hard to miss, but there may be large numbers of these great creatures feeding on plankton below the surface and therefore unknown. Because they are not likely to take a baited hook, the only ones that are seen are those that are sighted at the surface. Whale sharks are most frequently reported

from the Indian Ocean (between the Seychelles and Mauritius), off Southern California, the Philippines, in the Bay of Bengal, and off Taiwan.

Ningaloo Reef, off the coast of Western Australia, has become a destination for whale shark researchers, because it is a destination for whale sharks. The great sharks visit the reef between April and June. Although their appearance coincides with the annual coral spawn, the suggestion that they actually feed on the spawn has not been confirmed. The corals of Ningaloo breed once a year, after a full moon in March or April, spewing clouds of sperm and eggs into the tropical waters. Fertilization of the eggs then occurs in the water one or two hours later. Whale sharks eat by opening their large mouths and taking in the seawater that contains their food; the animals are trapped by filters and the excess water is pushed out through their gills. They are one of three known species of sharks that are filter feeders, the others being the basking shark and the megamouth shark.

In November 2005, a brand-new aquarium opened in Atlanta, Georgia, its $200 million price tag underwritten by Bernie Marcus, cofounder of the Home Depot megastores. In the six-million-gallon tank, the primary attraction was a pair of male whale sharks named Ralph and Norton, after characters in the old television show *The Honeymooners*. (The aquarium subsequently added two females named Alice and Trixie, after Ralph's and Norton's wives.) The sharks were caught off Taiwan and airlifted to Georgia. In a newspaper interview, Marcus said, "You know they come right to you, they're amazing. They're almost like puppies, little large puppies. They've grown one foot since they've been here, and we know they're about 15 feet now. Ralph is gonna end up being 40, 45 feet, maybe 50 feet, maybe 60, we don't know."

Unfortunately, in January 2007, Ralph ended up dead, of unknown causes, and Norton followed him five months later. Ignoring suggestions from biologists and aquarists that maybe the whale shark was ill suited to captivity, the aquarium replaced the two dead ones with two new males, Taroko and Yushan, flown in from Taiwan in June 2008. At the same time, the Georgia Aquarium announced a program that would allow selected visitors to swim with the whale sharks. Within a week of the announcement, 1,500 people signed up.

BASKING SHARK

After the whale shark, the basking shark is the world's second largest fish.

IN 1982, GAVIN MAXWELL, a man usually associated with otters (he wrote *Ring of Bright Water*), wrote, "The first clear and entire view of a basking shark is terrifying. One may speak glibly of fish twenty, thirty, forty feet long, but until one looks down upon a living adult basking shark in clear water, the figures are meaningless and without implication. The bulk appears simply unbelievable. It is not possible to think of what one is looking at as a fish. It is longer than a London bus; it does not have scales like an ordinary fish; its movements are gigantic, ponderous, and unfamiliar; it seems a creature from a prehistoric world, of which the first sight is as unexpected, and in some ways as shocking, as that of a dinosaur or iguanodon would be."

These words appeared in his first book, *Harpoon at a Venture* (1952),[†] which was a chronicle of Maxwell's experiences as a commercial shark fisherman in the waters of the Hebrides from 1945 to 1949. Maxwell fished for *Cetorhinus maximus*, the basking shark, because he believed that this enormous creature could provide enough liver oil to make a profitable industry for the island of Soay off the coast of Skye in Scotland, which he had purchased in 1946. (The liver of a single basking shark, sometimes as much as 20 percent of its total weight, might provide as much as five hundred gallons of oil.) The venture failed for many reasons, not the least of which concerned an attempt to utilize all the by-products of the shark, including the skin, the flesh, and the fins. In *Harpoon at a Venture*, we learn a great deal about the second largest fish in the world (Maxwell saw hundreds

† Since reprinted under the title *Harpoon Venture*.

of basking sharks during his four-year adventure and estimated the largest one at "upwards of forty feet").

Like the whale shark, the basking shark is a huge, slow-moving plankton feeder. Also like the whale shark, the basking shark is the sole member of a family created especially to accommodate it. The shark is called *Cetorhinus maximus*, and the family is Cetorhinidae. The name *Cetorhinus* comes from *cetos*, meaning "whale," and *rhiny*, meaning "shark" or "rasp." There is therefore the possibility that the scientific name of the basking shark, *Cetorhinus*, would be more appropriately given to the "whale shark," but it is best not to dwell too long on the exact translation of scientific names. In any event, the *maximus* part of the basking shark's name is clear: It means "great," and there is no dispute about that. One specimen, measuring twenty-nine feet, weighed in pieces at the Soay station totaled more than six tons, with the stomach contents estimated at another ton. Other documented weights for basking sharks are 6,580 pounds at twenty-eight feet and 8,600 pounds at thirty feet. In 1969, a twenty-seven-foot specimen weighing 4,400 pounds was captured by commercial fishermen in the Gulf of Mexico near Siesta Key, Florida. This, the first instance of a basking shark in the warm waters of the gulf, considerably extended its known range. For the most part, basking sharks are found in colder waters, primarily in the North Atlantic and the lower latitudes in northern and southern Pacific waters. It was long believed that these huge creatures lived in discrete local populations, but when a shark tagged off the Isle of Man appeared off Newfoundland, some six thousand miles away, the migratory habits of *Cetorhinus maximus* had to be reexamined. A transmitter affixed to this shark showed that it spent nights at depths of 600–900 feet, and once reached a depth of 4,145 feet.

In profile (but not in dentition) the basking shark is similar to the mackerel shark. It has a lunate caudal fin (which is a fancy way of saying that the tail fin is shaped like a crescent moon); a high, triangular dorsal fin; and a pointed snout. The eye of a basking shark is small, like the eye of a pig, which gives it a somewhat stupid-looking appearance. In its gross morphology, its enormous gill slits are its most dramatic feature. There are five, as in most sharks, and they extend the full height of the profile, almost meeting below the head. This gives the shark a most peculiar appearance, as if it were nearly decapitated.

The huge gill slits are extremely necessary to the shark's modus operandi, since it feeds on plankton by swimming through the water with its mouth and gills opened wide. On the inside of the gills is a series of long, quill-like gill rakers, which serve to trap minute animals and plants as water washes out through the gill slits. While feeding, the basking shark swims at a gentle speed of about two knots per hour. It eats and breathes simultaneously, as the water carrying the plankton also passes over the gill arches, which absorb the oxygen that the fish requires.

On rare occasions, basking sharks without gill rakers are taken. This infrequent occurrence has led to theories of hibernation (since the fish obviously cannot eat without its feeding apparatus) or annual replacement of the gill rakers. Some scientists feel that during periods when food is scarce, the sharks descend into deeper water for a protracted period of inactivity. At present, our knowledge of the habits of the basking shark is restricted to observations that can be made from the surface or from above. For instance, in the late 1940s a basking shark fishery off the coast of California used spotter planes to locate the sharks.

While mature basking sharks have ordinary-looking heads, some young specimens have snouts so long that they are said to resemble short trunks, often with a hornlike protuberance on the end. *Cetorhinus maximus* is usually said to be brownish or blackish in color, but Gavin Maxwell described them thus: "Looking down from the foredeck of a boat, the body never looks darker than the water surrounding it, always lighter and of an umberish color with darker markings." The shark's skin is covered with mucous (the purpose of which is not known), which dries to a blackish color when exposed to the air; this probably explains why the dorsal fin seen projecting above the surface of the water usually appears black to observers. This covering is unpleasant to touch and smells awful. The skin of the basking shark is covered with minute denticles, which, unlike those of most other sharks, seem to be arranged in a haphazard fashion. In other species, these dermal denticles point toward the tail, giving the fish a smoothness of texture when rubbed in that direction and the feeling of rough sandpaper when rubbed toward the head, or against the grain. On the basker, the skin is rough to the touch in every direction.

Heuvelmans, in *In the Wake of Sea-Serpents*, devotes an entire chapter to "all the stranded monsters that have proved to be basking sharks." There is a lengthy discussion of the "Stronsa Beast," a cause célèbre in 1808 and thereafter. It had washed up on the beach at Stronsa (now spelled Stronsay), in the Orkney Islands north of Scotland and was identified as a sea snake with a mane like that of a horse, a long neck, six legs, and a total length of some fifty-five feet. It was given the scientific name *Halsydurus maximus* ("great sea snake"); for a time, a new creature was known to the world. When sections of the vertebral column, parts of the skull, and pieces of the skin were examined, it became clear that *Halsydurus* was our old friend *Cetorhinus* after all. It seems that in decomposition, the basking shark leaves remains that can easily be mistaken for a sea monster: The great gill arches slough off first, leaving the small skull on the anterior end of the long vertebral column. The pectoral fins, pelvic fins, and claspers (the male's paired external genital organs) could all be mistaken for legs, and if the lower lobe of the tail rots off first—as it would tend to do, since vertebrae are only present in the upper lobe—it is quite possible to see the remains of a large basking shark as a sea monster. (The "mane like that of a horse" is probably the result of the fraying of the cartilaginous supports of the dorsal fins.) Occasionally, these mysterious remains are found at sea, giving even more credence to the possibility of sea serpents. In April 1977, a creature was found floating off New Zealand that seemed at first to defy identification. The "New Zealand Monster" was hauled up in the net of the Japanese mackerel trawler *Zuiyo Maru* and hoisted onto the deck. The ragged carcass, which was thirty-two feet long and weighed almost two tons, looked uncannily like a long-necked plesiosaur. After it was measured and photographed, pieces were snipped off for tissue samples, and it was dumped overboard so as not to contaminate the ship's catch. "It's not a fish, whale, or any other mammal," said Professor Yoshinori Imaizumi of the National Science Museum in Tokyo. But Dr. Bobb Schaeffer, a paleoichthyologist at the American Museum of Natural History in New York, said, "It's baloney. Every ten years or so something is found, usually in the Pacific, and people think it's a dinosaur. And it always turns out to be a basking shark or an adolescent whale." Alwyne Wheeler of the Natural History Museum in London agreed with his fellow ichthyologist and said it was the remains of a basking shark: "Sharks are cartilaginous fish. When they start to decompose after

death, the head and gills are the first to drop from the body.... Greater experts than the Japanese fishermen have been foiled by the similarity of shark remains to a plesiosaur."

Despite what appears to have been a great desire to identify the carcass as that of a sea monster, it turned out to be a basking shark after all. Before the carcass was discarded, one of the crewmen lopped off a piece of a fin. It contained the horny fibers (ceratorichia) that characterize the elasmobranchs, and these were later identified as those of *Cetorhinus maximus*. Still, if you squint at the photographs taken by a fisheries inspector aboard the *Zuiyo Maru*, the carcass looks a lot more like a rotten dinosaur than an old, dead shark.

It had been long recognized that the two largest fish in the world were the whale shark and the basking shark, both harmless plankton eaters. Then—out of the blue, as it were—another cartilaginous plankton eater appeared; at fourteen feet it was not quite in the same class as the whale shark or the basker, but it was a very big fish nonetheless.

MEGAMOUTH SHARK

In November 1976, just as the first edition of my *Book of Sharks* was going to press, Peter Benchley called to tell me he had heard that they had "found a Megalodon." In a state of near hysteria, I called CBS News, because Benchley said that Walter Cronkite had announced it on his news program—if true, it would change the swimming habits of the world forever. I finally discovered that Cronkite had said "megamouth," not "Megalodon," but that was news enough. In the shark book, I had written, "For every species that is synonymized, there is probably a new one already discovered, or waiting to be discovered." Still, I had not expected a major new species to be discovered within a month of the book's publication. I could not get megamouth into the first printing, but I managed to correct the oversight in subsequent editions.

It seems that the *AFB-14*, a naval research vessel operating in deep water off the northern coast of the Hawaiian island of Oahu, had deployed two orange-and-white parachutes as sea anchors, and when they hauled them in, the crew discovered that one of them had been swallowed by a very large shark. Parachute-eating sharks are remarkable enough, but this creature was more than a little unusual: It was of a type totally unrecognizable to the crew. More than fourteen feet long, the huge-mouthed creature weighed three-quarters of a ton. It had thousands of tiny teeth, and its rubbery lips made it look more like a seagoing hippopotamus than a shark. The sea anchor had been deployed at about five hundred feet, which suggests that this was a deepwater plankton feeder and therefore a fish that

Megamouth, a 14-foot-long harmless shark that was unknown until 1976, when one swallowed a parachute sea anchor five hundred feet down off the Hawaiian island of Oahu.

would have been unlikely to have taken a baited hook. Were it not for the pure coincidence of the ship and the shark being in the same place at the same time—and the bizarre inclination of the shark to swallow the chute—this animal might never have been discovered.

It was not until 1984 that a second specimen, also a male, was caught off Southern California. A third male washed ashore in Western Australia in 1988, and a fourth, a badly decomposed male, was discovered in January 1989, washed ashore in Japan. Six months later, another decomposed male was found in Japan. The first living megamouth, number six, was not seen until October 21, 1990, when a commercial fisherman snagged one in his gill net seven miles off Dana Point, California. He brought the fifteen-foot male into the harbor, where ichthyologists marveled at it and television crews filmed it for science, posterity, and publicity. Since no aquarium had the facilities to exhibit this creature, the authorities wisely and sensitively decided to release it. On October 23, the shark, dubbed "Mega" by the media, was returned to the Pacific.

In May 1995, an immature male, only six feet long, was found on the beach in Senegal, and six months after that, the first Atlantic megamouth was found in Brazil. Numbers ten and eleven were found in Japan and the Philippines, respectively; number twelve, the only known mature female at seventeen feet nine inches, was also found in Japan (her right ovary possessed a large number of whitish yellow eggs). Number thirteen was not collected at all but observed offshore, north of the city of Manado on the Indonesian island of Sulawesi (once known as Celebes), being harassed by sperm whales. In October 1999, a large female (seventeen feet) was caught in a drift net off San Diego, California, photographed, and released. Two years later, a large male (eighteen feet) was entrapped in a drift gill net, hauled on deck and photographed, and then thrown overboard. Megamouth number sixteen was an immature male caught in a tuna purse seine in the eastern Indian Ocean in January 2002. In April of that year the first South African megamouth, which became number seventeen, was stranded at Natures Valley in the Western Cape Province. Number eighteen came from the Philippines; number nineteen was sighted at sea off California; and number twenty was caught on July 4, 2003, off Taiwan.

The first megamouth from the eastern south Atlantic was

number twenty-two, found off Peru in March 2004, and in the same month, number twenty-three washed ashore at Gapang Beach, off the northern tip of the Indonesian island of Sumatra. The next specimens (numbers twenty-four and twenty-five) came from Japan in April 2004; one was discovered floating in Tokyo Bay near Ichihara City: At a length of eighteen feet six inches and a weight of 2,679 pounds, it is the largest megamouth yet reported. Number twenty-six was discovered stranded alive on the beach of the coastal village of Barangay Namocon on Panay Island in the Philippines, and died a couple of hours later. In January 2005, megamouth number twenty-seven was captured in a purse seine off the east coast of Japan. Representatives of the nearby Toba Aquarium rushed to the scene, hoping to be able to take the living shark to their facility, but when they arrived, the shark—a female seventeen feet four inches long—had died. Megamouth number twenty-eight was found dead in Cagayan de Oro, Philippines. Numbers twenty-nine through thirty-three were all caught by Taiwanese fishermen in the spring of 2005, and in January 2006, a large specimen was seen struggling to free itself from a fishing net just off Bayawan City on Negros Island in the Philippines. Two months later number thirty-five, a large female, was trapped in a net and died in Macajalar Bay on the north coast of Mindanao Island. Megamouth number thirty-six was caught in Sagami Bay, on the east coast of Japan, in May 2006.

From these specimens, we have learned that megamouth is a flabby creature with an enormous mouth, blubbery lips, and thousands of tiny teeth, indicating that it is a plankton feeder. Indeed, when the stomach contents of stranded specimens were examined, nothing larger than copepods and shrimps were found. Megamouth number six, the first living specimen, was outfitted for two days with an acoustic transmitter, and biologists under the leadership of Don Nelson learned that this shark spent the daytime hours between 400 and 550 feet (confirmed by the first megamouth specimen having swallowed a parachute at 500 feet), migrating to within 40 feet of the surface at night. It is likely that the shark's vertical migrations are coordinated with the fluctuating depth of the so-called deep-scattering layer (DSL), a horizontal, mobile zone of living organisms that occurs below the surface in many oceans and is called "scattering" because it is so dense that it scatters or reflects sound waves.

Throughout Hawaiian history—from the early days of the

Polynesian sailing canoes, through the Pacific explorers of the eighteenth and nineteenth centuries, and past World War II in the Pacific (when there was considerable naval action off Hawaii)—no hint of the existence of this fish had ever appeared. No megamouth had ever been recorded in Japan until eleven specimens appeared between 1989 and 2006; and the six Philippine specimens (1998–2006) were apparently the first ever seen there. Much is weird and peculiar about the megamouth shark, but it is incredible that the species was undiscovered until 1976, and since then, thirty-five additional specimens have washed ashore or been captured in nets around the world. Where were they and what were they doing before 1976?

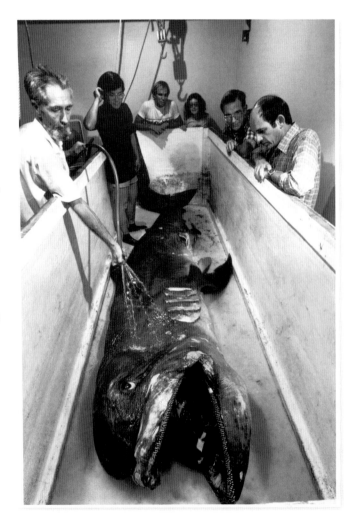

Scientists examine the first megamouth in the Bishop Museum, Honolulu. Leighton R. Taylor, who would eventually describe the shark for science, is in the right foreground.

GREAT WHITE SHARK

When I received a phone call from the local fishermen in Rhode Island (I had left a note asking to be notified if any sharks were brought in), I asked what kind of shark they had found and was told that it was "just a gray shark." I almost said that I was not interested in "just a gray shark" (which I thought would be a blue shark or a sandbar shark), but since they had taken the trouble to call, I felt I ought to pay them the courtesy of responding. When I arrived at the docks, I asked where the "man-eater" was, knowing that it was no such thing. The fishermen indicated that it was behind a pile of boxes on the pier, and when I saw it, I gave an involuntary start—it was a man-eater, a great white shark. Four feet two inches long, it weighed fifty-one pounds. When I explained that this was indeed a white shark, I was told that I had probably seen *Jaws* too recently: White sharks were huge monsters, there were no white sharks in Rhode Island, and how did I know, anyway?

I pointed out the characteristics that identified this as a great white and no other species: The snout was conical, not flattened. The teeth were triangular, serrated, and proportionally large. (In this four-foot specimen, the largest tooth measured just under three-quarters of an inch in length; in the largest specimens, the teeth are more than two inches long.) The eye was black with no visible pupil; the fish itself was a dark gray brown, and its undersides were white. On the lower surface, the pectoral fins were tipped with black, and at the axil (corresponding to the human armpit), there was an oval black spot. At the base of the tail were the flattened keels that are characteristic of the family, and the upper and lower lobes of the tail were almost equal in size. (The other members of the family are the mako and the porbeagle, but their teeth are different, their pectorals are not black-tipped, and they have no axillar spot.)

The great white shark, *Carcharodon carcharias*, even at the age of a few months, is larger than many other full-grown species. It is a completely functional apex predator, a perfect small-scale version of the massive creature it will become. Its diet consists largely of tuna, other sharks, rays, dolphins, porpoises, seals, sea lions, and whale carcasses, and nothing else in the water preys on it. Once you have seen a great white, you will never mistake it for any other shark.

Because of the hyperbolic nature of many descriptions of the white shark, the maximum size records are full of misinformation, typographic errors, and wild exaggerations. When a fish weighs more than a ton, as large white sharks do, it is a difficult proposition to weigh it at all, let alone to weigh it accurately. Very few docks are equipped with the scales necessary to perform this task, and it is understandably difficult

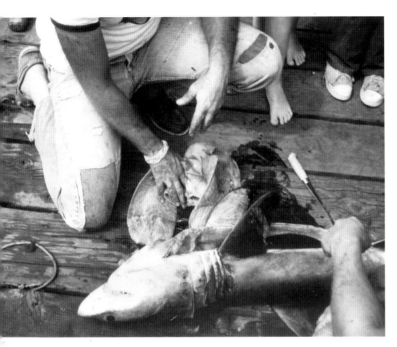

The author dissects a 4-foot-long newborn white shark, which had drowned in a fisherman's net off Little Compton, Rhode Island.

to transport the fish to a location where there is a scale equal to the job. We therefore find that the weight of many of the larger whites has been guessed or estimated using some length-girth-weight formula that is often not revealed. For example, the shark that Frank Mundus harpooned off Montauk, Long Island, in 1964 (which, incidentally, was one of the "real" elements that Peter Benchley incorporated into his novel *Jaws*), was reported to have weighed 4,500 pounds. The sign that accompanies the mounted head of this specimen in Salivar's Dock, a restaurant in Montauk, gives this as the unequivocal weight. It seems curious that it is such a round number, and we discover from Mundus's own book, *Sportfishing for Sharks* (1971), that the fish was never weighed at all. It was only measured, and then the "tonnage" was estimated, "based on known length-girth-weight relationships." I have seen this head, and there is no question that it was an enormous fish—it was seventeen feet long and thirteen feet in girth. The figure of 4,500 pounds, however, has entered the literature without the fish ever having been weighed.

The largest recorded great whites include Mundus's 1964 specimen; a fifteen-foot, 3,031-pound female caught in California in 1958; a 2,875-pound fish harpooned off Peru; and two specimens, 3,150 and 3,440 pounds, harpooned during the summer of 1975 off the California coast. All of the largest specimens were females; females are usually larger than males. (Both of the 1975 California specimens had substantial prey animals in them when they were examined; the larger one had the "posterior quarter of a northern elephant seal present.") The largest fish ever caught on rod and reel was a white shark weighing 2,664 pounds, by Alf Dean off Ceduna, Australia, on April 21, 1959. When fishing for white sharks, they are chummed alongside the boat with whale oil, fish, and blood. They are also fed hunks of horsemeat or sheep in an attempt to get them to take the hook. There is a question as to whether the record fish are weighed with or without the chum, or if a shark with a

four-hundred-pound seal in it should have that added to its total weight.

Off Albany, Western Australia, in April 1976, Clive Green caught a sixteen-foot female *Carcharodon* that was weighed at 3,388 pounds. Although considerable publicity attended this feat of angling (a line manufacturer again hailed it as "the largest fish ever caught on rod and reel"), it was not allowed as the world's record. One of the rules of the International Game Fish Association (IGFA), which superintends world-record catches, is that a catch will be disqualified if "the flesh, blood, skin, or any part of mammals" is used for chumming or bait. (The idea is to discourage illegal use of dolphins or other mammals.) Since Green used whale meat as bait, his record was disqualified. In August 1986, Donnie Braddick, fishing out of Montauk with Captain Mundus, caught another white shark that a line manufacturer also proclaimed "the largest fish ever taken on rod and reel." The fish does not appear in the 1987 IGFA record book, although the line manufacturer's ad does. According to the ad, the fish was seventeen feet long and weighed 3,427 pounds. There seems to be no question about the shark's size, but a question about the way in which it was caught resulted in its disqualification. The fishermen had tied their boat to a whale carcass, which meant that they too were guilty of using "any part of mammals . . . for trolling or casting," and like Green's, Braddick's giant fish did not enter the official record book. (Dean's 1959 world-record white shark was caught with "porpoise" as bait, but this record has been allowed to stand because the shark was caught before the rule concerning mammals was introduced.) What is the largest white shark on record? In his 1987 "Refutation of Lengths of 11.3, 9.0, and 6.4 m Attributed to the White Shark, *Carcharodon carcharias*," Jack Randall quotes Gordon Hubbell (a Miami veterinarian and collector of white shark teeth, jaws, and data) as saying that the largest white shark he knows of is a nineteen-foot six-inch female caught off Western Australia in 1984. This monster weighed 3,324 pounds and was neither caught on rod and reel nor harpooned; it was *lassoed* by Fisheries Officer Colin Ostle off Ledge Point, near Albany.

The number of very large white sharks said to have been caught or sighted is enormous (in part, because they seem to be found off every coast in the temperate seas), but some of these are apocryphal, some are imaginary, and some are simply wild

PREVIOUS SPREAD *No escape for a sea lion in the curl of a California wave.*
OPPOSITE *Great white shark. Is this the most dangerous fish in the world?*

exaggerations. (In their *Fishes of the Western North Atlantic*, Henry B. Bigelow and William C. Schroeder recount the story of "an Australian specimen, reported in the local newspapers as 16 feet long, [that] actually measured only eight feet six inches.") Quite often the size of the shark is exaggerated beyond all rational bounds, probably because the viewer has no idea how large this fish is supposed to get. When the maximum size of the white shark was generally accepted as exceeding thirty-five feet, sightings of twenty-five-footers did not seem that remarkable. In his *Living Fishes of the World*, Earl Herald—a respected ichthyologist whose book was published in 1961, before Perry Gilbert examined the Port Fairy jaws in the British Museum—wrote, "The largest man-eater ever caught measured 36.5 feet in length and was taken at Port Fairey [*sic*], Australia. Although it dates back more than ninety years, the jaws have been preserved intact in the collection of the British Museum. In contrast with this giant, most of the man-eaters caught today are in the 20- to 25-foot range. Because of the thickness of the body, these sharks are massive fish. For example, a small shark 17 feet long can weigh as much as 2,800 pounds."

What about those jaws in the British Museum? When the Port Fairy jaws were actually measured, they were found to have come from a seventeen-foot specimen. We now know that a seventeen-foot great white shark is anything but "small," and in fact is fairly close to the maximum confirmed length. We know, too, that there have been seventeen-footers that have weighed more than four thousand pounds.

The largest white sharks accurately measured range between nineteen and twenty-one feet, and there are some questionable twenty-three-footers in the popular—but not the scientific—literature. These giants seem to disappear or shrink when a responsible observer approaches with a tape measure. The length of a shark is often calculated by measuring a submerged shark against the boat in which the observer sits, a dubious method at best. In his book *Shark for Sale* (1961), an account of his shark-fishing experiences in the Seychelles, William Travis tells of hooking a huge shark that was hauled up "foot by foot" to "see how tired the brute was." By measuring the shark against a mark scratched on the bulwark of his shark-fishing boat, Travis concluded that the fish was twenty-nine feet long. The brute was not very tired, however, because it "made a determined

dash ahead, swung round the anchor chain, baulked as the line caught on it, and then, with one savage lunge of its head, snapped the rope as if it were a strand of cotton." Until someone verifies anything more than twenty-one feet—a record that has stood since 1948 (and even this one is open to doubt)—we shall accept that figure as the maximum known size for the great white shark. But even at a paltry nineteen feet, a great white can weigh as much as a rhinoceros, and that is a very big fish indeed.

The great white is the shark most often implicated in attacks on humans, and it is always number one on the list of dangerous sharks or man-eaters. People have died as a result of white shark attacks, but very few have actually been eaten, either whole or in part. Perhaps this is splitting hairs, but I believe that it is necessary to draw a distinction between death as a result of excessive bleeding after being attacked by a shark and death as a result of having a portion of one's anatomy ripped off and swallowed. Researchers on the subject of shark attacks are interested in this distinction, since the discovery of the motive of a shark attack is necessary to its prevention.

Of the thirty-two recorded white shark attacks, an incredible 37.5 percent occurred on a stretch of the California coastline less than 120 miles long (measured in a straight line between two terminal points). This zone centers on San Francisco, extending from Tomales Point at Bodega Bay in the north to Santa Cruz to Monterey Bay in the south, and includes the Farallon Islands, about thirty miles west of the city, a popular area for abalone diving and the home of a colony of sea lions. It appears that if San Francisco were to slide into the sea, as some predict it will, there would be even more to worry about than mere earthquakes, fires, and tidal waves. According to the statistics, the city and its environs have easily won the unwanted title of White Shark Attack Capital of the World. South Australia is a poor second, with four attacks by white sharks, only one of which was fatal. Of the twelve attacks that have taken place in California, two resulted in the death of the victim. Most of these attacks occurred in Northern California, but on April 26, 2008, David Martin, a sixty-six-year-old retired veterinarian, was swimming with a triathalon training group off Solana Beach, north of San Diego, when a great white shark attacked him, biting him so severely on the legs that he bled to death.

The number of survivors of attacks by great whites—about

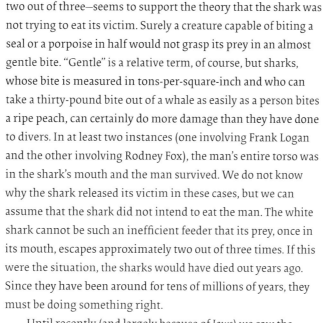

two out of three—seems to support the theory that the shark was not trying to eat its victim. Surely a creature capable of biting a seal or a porpoise in half would not grasp its prey in an almost gentle bite. "Gentle" is a relative term, of course, but sharks, whose bite is measured in tons-per-square-inch and who can take a thirty-pound bite out of a whale as easily as a person bites a ripe peach, can certainly do more damage than they have done to divers. In at least two instances (one involving Frank Logan and the other involving Rodney Fox), the man's entire torso was in the shark's mouth and the man survived. We do not know why the shark released its victim in these cases, but we can assume that the shark did not intend to eat the man. The white shark cannot be such an inefficient feeder that its prey, once in its mouth, escapes approximately two out of three times. If this were the situation, the sharks would have died out years ago. Since they have been around for tens of millions of years, they must be doing something right.

Until recently (and largely because of *Jaws*) we saw the great white as some sort of primordial terror, indiscriminately attacking swimmers, divers, and boats—a marine homicidal maniac that ought to be eliminated from the world's oceans so it would not kill everybody. Our fear of the great white has begun to dissipate, because we have been able to see them not as killers, but as part of the complex web of life in the ocean. The revised view has come about partly because juvenile white sharks, caught off Southern California, have been placed on display in the Monterey Bay Aquarium, where viewers can watch them gliding gracefully among the other fish (mostly tuna, larger and heavier than the seven-foot-long sharks), apparently impervious to their surroundings and not at all threatening to divers who enter the tank. To date, two little great whites have been exhibited at Monterey. Their sabbatical in tanks notwithstanding, however, great white sharks are still very big, very dangerous fish. The exhibition of juveniles will not dull the razorlike

serrations of their teeth, nor will it change the centuries of calumny the white shark has endured.

Captain Frank Mundus (left) with the fisherman who caught this 14-foot-long great white off Montauk, Long Island.

MAKO SHARK

THE MAKO (*Isurus paucus* and *I. oxyrinchus*)[†] is the quintessential shark. It is probably the most graceful of all sharks: the most beautifully proportioned, the fastest, and the most strikingly colored. It is a spectacular game fish and one of the meanest-looking animals on earth. Like its close relatives in the Lamnidae family, the great white and the porbeagle, it is gracefully streamlined, with a conical snout, small second dorsal fins, and a homocercal tail (that is, one where the upper and lower fins are symmetrical) with a pair of horizontally flattened keels at the tail's base. Sharks in this family, called isurids, or lamnids, or mackerel sharks, possess dark eyes that give them a look of intense intelligence that they may not possess, reminiscent of another group of superbly designed predators: the falcons.

Another characteristic that separates the isurids from all other elasmobranchs is their ability to conserve heat and maintain a body temperature that is considerably higher than the ambient water. It had long been known that certain scombroid fish, especially tuna, have this ability, but in 1968 two Woods Hole Oceanographic Institution biologists, Francis G. Carey and John M. Teal, were the first to mention this phenomenon in sharks. Only makos and porbeagles were tested, but white sharks, the third member of the family, were examined and showed the same structural modifications—so it is safe to assume that they share this ability. According to Carey and Teal, heat is conserved by a "set of countercurrent heat exchangers located in the circulation between the gills and the tissues. The heat exchangers form a thermal barrier which permits the flow of blood but blocks the flow of heat." The authors conclude that there is a threefold increase in the muscle power for every ten degrees centigrade rise in body temperature. And muscle power is what a

mako shark needs: A fish this size that can jump fifteen to twenty feet in the air requires a starting velocity of twenty-two miles per hour. In a popular book on sharks, I read that makos can catch swordfish "capable of speeds up to 60 miles an hour," but this seems a bit excessive for both shark and swordfish.

Almost all sharks are dark above and lighter below, but few show the dramatic contrast between the rich ultramarine dorsal surface and snowy underbelly of the mako, often separated by a band of silver. A profile portrait of the mako shows this shark to best advantage, emphasizing the conical snout, which is so uniquely pointed. This characteristic has resulted in one of its vernacular names: sharpnose mackerel shark. Other common names include blue pointer, mackerel shark, and bonito shark. Makos have particularly long teeth, but they are not serrated like those of their infamous cousin, the great white, nor are they cusped like those of their relative, the porbeagle. The teeth of a big mako are huge, resembling curved knives set into the jaw. They are also flattened on the forward surface, which increases this knifelike impression. Smaller specimens have more rounded teeth, so it takes a big mako to display the full and frightening implications of these teeth. The teeth of most sharks are laid back when not in use, and the opening of the mouth brings them into an upright position. This occurs to a limited extent with the mako, but its lower teeth are always erect and serve to give this shark, in life as well as in death, a snaggletoothed and fearful visage.

For the big-game fisherman, however, mako fishing is the stuff of which dreams are made. Capable of spectacular gymnastics and, at the same time, one of the few fish whose actions can be decidedly aggressive, the mako brings an added dimension to game fishing. Makos charge boats, sometimes jump right into them, and generally provide a level of excitement beyond that of the ordinary game-fish experience. In mako fishing, not only might you lose your fish, but also your rod or even your arm. It is perhaps the only type of big-game fishing where there is a real element of personal danger.

It is difficult at best to judge heights from the water, but there seems to be a general consensus that a fighting mako

† There are two known mako sharks, the longfin mako (*Isurus paucus*) and the shortfin mako (*Isurus oxyrinchus*). They are both large fish and are not differentiated in most accounts.

can jump at least twenty feet in the air. For the May–June 1934 issue of *Natural History* magazine, Zane Grey wrote an article titled "The Great Mako." In a prefatory note, Dr. E. W. Gudger said, "It is the first account ever published … of a shark that leaps when it is hooked." The photographs accompanying the article, "illustrate for the first time this leaping fighter of the South Seas." Anyone who has ever tried to anticipate the spot from which a hooked fish will emerge from the water will understand the difficulties involved and realize that, for 1934, these photographs are spectacular. (In fact, they are pretty good even for today—I have not seen many better photographs of leaping makos.) Grey did his mako fishing in New Zealand waters, particularly off North Island, and prior to his much-publicized exploits, sharks had not been considered game fish at all. Then, for many years, the mako was the only shark on the International Game Fish Association's list, but now six more species are included: the blue, the porbeagle, the hammerhead, the thresher, the tiger, and the white.

Makos are worldwide in distribution, favoring tropical and temperate waters. They do not school and they are never seen in very large numbers. One area in which they seem to be fairly plentiful is the Atlantic Ocean just south of Long Island, New York. For many years, the Bay Shore Tuna Club has held a mako tournament there, and the catch, while never as plentiful as the blue sharks or the sandbars, has not been insignificant. For example, in 1975 there were 50 makos, 120 blues, and 110 sandbars caught. Makos are also caught off the coasts of England, as related by Trevor Housby in *The Rubby-Dubby Trail: Shark Fishing in British Waters* (1972). ("Rubby-dubby" is the equivalent of chum, only it is not ladled overboard, but rather hung in the water in a cheesecloth bag to disperse an oil slick.) Housby discusses only four species of sharks: the porbeagle, the blue, the thresher, and the mako. Makos in British waters seem to attain a respectable size; the current record is a five-hundred-pounder caught by a Mrs. Yallop off Looe in Cornwall, and Housby tells of even larger fish that were hooked but got away before they could be brought to gaff.

The mako is always included in lists of potentially dangerous sharks, even though the number of authenticated reports of unprovoked attacks seems to be quite low. In the International Shark Attack File, a database of all known shark attacks, a total of eighteen attacks are attributed to makos, but as David Baldridge says, "More often than not, identifications were made on the weakest of evidence, and were … no more than snap judgements made by casual observers." Like the porbeagle, the mako tends to inhabit deeper waters than the great white—another way of saying that there have been fewer recorded instances of makos in the vicinity of swimmers. In the category of "attacks on boats," the mako is the undisputed leader, according to J. A. F. Garrick and Leonard P. Schultz in "Potentially Dangerous Sharks," an essay published in *Sharks and Survival* (1963).

White sharks feed on seals and sea lions as well as fish, and these marine mammals are often found close to shore. Makos and porbeagles are piscivorous, and they habituate the areas where their prey is found. Makos, especially, seem to have a particular affinity for the flesh of billfish, especially the swordfish. There are numerous records of makos caught with a broken sword of a marlin or a swordfish in their flesh, and in one case an entire swordfish weighing 120 pounds was found in the stomach of a 730-pound mako.

The world-record makos come from New Zealand waters, although there seem to be good-size specimens throughout their range. (The word *mako* is of Maori origin; its derivation is unclear, although it is probably not, as has been suggested, a corruption of the English word "mackerel.") During his three seasons in New Zealand, Zane Grey caught "in the neighborhood of seventy makos." He kept careful records, and his largest weighed 580 pounds, of which he says, "The last began to get into a class with big mako." The all-tackle mako record, listed in the IGFA Record Book, is a 1,061-pound, twelve-foot-two-inch-long fish caught off Mayor Island, New Zealand. Records such as this indicate only fish brought to gaff under strict IGFA regulations; there are a lot of bigger fish that are not successfully boated. As Grey put it, "The mako is a fish that often gets away." Reliable estimates of the largest makos run to a weight of 1,300-plus pounds, and a length of more than thirteen feet.

OPPOSITE *The porbeagle is smaller and stockier than its better-known relatives, the mako and the great white. It is characterized by a white spot at the base of the dorsal fin.*

LEFT *Portrait of a mako, with teeth Hemingway described as "crisped like claws."*

RIGHT *Although it looks like it is flying at 20,000 feet, this mako is leaping out of the water. The horizon is just out of sight.*

THRESHER SHARK

The tail of the thresher shark, as long as the shark itself, may be used to corral baitfish into a tight formation so the shark can feed on them.

IN 1887, J. W. BUEL PUBLISHED A BOOK called *Sea and Land: An Illustrated History of the Wonderful and Curious Things of Nature Existing Before and Since the Deluge. A Natural History of the Sea, Land Creatures, the Cannibals, and Wild Races of the World*. From its title, one can deduce that this eight-hundred-page book is going to be filled with wild tales of human/animal (and human/human) interactions, most of which are the result of accumulated folklore, and almost all of which are either incorrect, or such wild exaggerations that they do not even make sense. Here, for example, is his account of "the thrasher or fox shark": "In my remarks about whales, I have alluded to the habit of the fox-shark combining with the grampus in attacks upon the whale, which they kill. The fox-shark is not only a formidable antagonist of the whale, but also ferociously attacks other monsters of the deep, such as seals, porpoises, lamantins [manatees], etc., and has killed many a shipwrecked sailor by the wild lashings of its terrible tail, out of pure wantonness, for it is not known to eat man."

According to the folktales, the thresher's interaction with whales includes a third party, the swordfish. It seems that the thresher would circle the unlucky whale, slapping at the water with its sicklelike tail, beating the surface of the ocean into a froth to confuse the victim. While the whale was thus distracted, the swordfish would pierce the hapless whale in a vital spot and kill it. This cooperative venture was apparently undertaken because neither the thresher nor the swordfish could handle the large

whale separately. The results of this cooperation would appear to be a cetacean feast for the participants.

Unfortunately, neither the swordfish nor the thresher includes whale meat in its regular diet, so this whole operation seems rather unnecessary, if not downright wasteful. The fable does point up an interesting comparison between the alleged coconspirators: Both have an abnormally elongated appendage, the swordfish in the forward position and the thresher in the aft. We have a pretty good idea of the uses the swordfish (or the marlin or the sailfish) makes of its elongated snout, but the thresher's tail is a little more problematic. Generally, the tail is about equal in length to the body of the fish, and since a thresher can achieve a total length of twenty feet, that means ten feet of shark and ten feet of tail. Among the uses suggested for this tail are the following, in descending order of credibility: It is used to round up fish into a compact school, which the shark then feeds on; it is used to flip fish out of the water and into its mouth; it is used to slap seabirds sitting on the surface, so the shark can then gobble up the stunned birds. There are "eyewitness" reports of these actions, and somewhat less well-documented stories about truly bizarre uses to which the tail has been put. One story, quoted by someone who relates the tale secondhand, tells of a longline fisherman who had hooked a large shark. When he leaned over the gunwale to see his catch, the tail of a thresher came whipping out of the water and decapitated him.

Most sharks have only one offensive apparatus: their mouths. Even sharks with relatively small teeth (like threshers), use these teeth to capture their prey, to fight, or to defend themselves. It is therefore somewhat surprising to hear, even in theory, of a shark that uses its tail as a food-gathering device or as an offensive weapon. The only other higher animals I can think of that use their tails for anything other than hanging from trees, brushing off flies, or wagging as some sort of an instinctive signal (as with dogs and deer), are crocodiles and porcupines. Crocodiles have been known to sweep their victims into the water with a swipe of their powerful tails and porcupines swing their quill-studded tails in defense against predators. Both these animals use their tails in the air, where resistance is considerably less than in the water. This is not to say that threshers do not use their tails as weapons or as food-gathering devices, but proof is sorely lacking. Threshers are usually found offshore, and I do not think their

feeding process has ever been observed, except at the surface and from a distance.

We know that a shark's source of propulsive power is its tail, the other fins serving as planing, stabilizing, or steering devices, so some connection must be drawn between the threshers' extraordinary appendages and their forward motion. If the tail is strong enough to accomplish even some of the wondrous feats ascribed to it, then it surely must add to the shark's speed. It may also have something to do with a "circling" motion; even if thresher sharks do not actually herd their prey—menhaden, shad, herring, or mackerel—into tightly packed schools, the fish adopt this defense on their own, and it may be advantageous to have the ability to circle tightly around a small school when feeding. The sharks definitely catch their prey with their teeth, not their tails, although the fact that they are often hooked in the upper lobe of the tailfin lends some credence to the idea that they use their tails to stun their prey.

There are three species of threshers. The best-known is the common thresher, *Alopias vulpinus* (whose names mean "fox fox" in Greek and Latin, respectively—names presumably derived from its long tail). Long believed to be just a kind of sooty brown above and white below, this species is actually the most brightly colored of all sharks. Where the mako and the blue shark are dark indigo on the back, the thresher is purple to violet, which fades into sky blue before becoming the silvery white of its undersides. The pelagic thresher, *A. pelagicus*, has smaller teeth than the common thresher and is found farther offshore, as its name suggests (*pélagos* is Greek for "open sea" and a pelagic species will not normally be found close to a coastline). The bigeye thresher (*A. super-ciliosus*), the deepwater member of the triumvirate, has fewer teeth in the jaws and a dorsal fin set much farther back. As befits its common name, the bigeye has huge eyes, which are said to be the largest eyes in proportion to its body of any nonavian vertebrate. These enormous eyes are positioned nearer to the top of the head (the dorsal surface) than those of any other shark, suggesting that the shark needs to look up in its deepwater habitat. The head is defined by a deep, angled groove that begins just in front of the eyes and ends at the gill slits. Because of their distinctive appearance, threshers have been given a variety of colorful and descriptive names, including fox shark, foxtail, swiveltail, and sickletail.

The range of the thresher is enormous: It inhabits coastal and oceanic waters around the world, absent only in the higher polar latitudes. Given their wide-ranging habits, threshers are not common anywhere, and thus the surface species (common and pelagic) are considered prime game fish wherever they are found and they receive regular mention in books about big-game fishing in New England, California, Australia, and of course, New Zealand. All species are susceptible to longline fisheries, and their meat and fins are eagerly consumed, especially in Asian countries.

Most of the heavy-tackle specimens come from New Zealand, while the light-tackle specimens have been caught in California waters. The current record for the common thresher is a 767-pounder, caught in the Bay of Islands, New Zealand, in 1983. It was fifteen feet five inches long. Earlier records show a 922-pound specimen, also from New Zealand, but this one was caught on untested line and is therefore ineligible for the record books. The bigeye thresher, a recent entry into the IGFA record book, tops the common thresher record; one caught at Tutukaka, New Zealand, in 1981 weighed 802 pounds. Zane Grey, writing about the thresher in New Zealand waters, called it "exceedingly stubborn. Comparing him with the mako, he is pound for pound, a harder fish to whip."

A most unfortunate demonstration of the "*Jaws* mentality" occurred late in the summer of 2007, when a seriously debilitated, half-grown thresher was spotted floundering in the surf off Rockaway Beach in Queens, New York. A panic ensued, with people running back and forth, shouting "Shark! Shark!," just as in the movie. When the poor creature washed ashore dead the next day, the headlines screamed, GET OUT OF THE WATER! and JAWS TERRIFIES ROCKAWAYS. The *New York Post* graced its front page with a portrait of the dead shark, showing a mouthful of tiny teeth that would not seem terrifying in a kitten. Even though the thresher is harmless—especially, as in this case, a sick one—a full-fledged panic gripped the beachgoers, and they were happy to be out of the water, because, as one of them said, "I didn't want to get eaten."

The bigeye thresher, a deep-water variation, has eyes that are aimed upward and a strange muscular construction behind the head.

TIGER SHARK

ACCORDING TO LEONARD COMPAGNO's *Sharks of the World* (2005), there are 453 species of sharks. The great majority of these do not qualify for inclusion in this book, for they are anything but big. Many are less than four feet long, and there are some deepwater species that barely reach two feet in length. But many species of sharks are fairly big; larger and heavier than a full-grown man, and based on size alone, many sharks are considered potential "man-eaters." We have already made the acquaintance of most of the lamnids, the group that includes the basking, megamouth, great white, mako, and thresher, as well as the porbeagle (*Lamna nasus*, twelve feet) and the salmon shark (*L. ditropis*, less than ten feet). Size has nothing to do with this classification, but all these species are sizable.

Sharks in the family Carcharhinidae can also be quite sizable. According to Compagno, the carcharhinids are, "active strong swimmers … some of them are 'ram-ventilators' needing to swim constantly to oxygenate their gills, others can rest on the bottom…. Long, arched mouth with bladelike teeth (often broader in upper jaw)… Usually round (to horizontal) eyes with internal nictitating eyelids… two dorsal fins, one anal fin, first dorsal medium to large, second usually much smaller…. These are major predators, taking a wide range of prey… several species are potentially harmful, having bitten people and boats…." This group of sharks was once known as the "requiem" sharks, although the origin of that term is vague. A "requiem" (from the Latin *requiés*, for "rest") is a Mass for the dead, so it is possible to say that these sharks kill people, ergo *requiem sharks*. Possible, but alas, not true. The French word for shark (of any kind) is *requin*, so it is easy to see how the words became conflated.

Carcharhinids are found throughout the world's oceans,

mostly but not exclusively in shallower, near-shore waters. Of the sixty-odd carcharhinid species, the better-known are the dusky shark (*Carcharhinus obscurus*, maximum length 12 feet); the sandbar shark (*C. plumbeus*, 11 feet); Galápagos shark (*C. galapgensis*, 11 feet); silky shark (*C. falciformis*, 10.5 feet); lemon shark (*Negaprion brevirostris*, 10 feet); Caribbean reef shark (*C. perezii*, 9.5 feet); bronze whaler (*C. brachyurus*, 9.5 feet); grey reef shark (*C. amblyrhynchos*, 8.5 feet); and the spinner shark (*C. brevipinna*, 8 feet.) All the carcharhinid species together comprise the bulk of the larger, more familiar sharks, and because most sportfishing takes place not far from shore, these are the sharks most often seen by nonichthyologists and nonlongliners. But among the carcharhinids, the really big fish are the tiger shark (*Galeocerdo cuvier*), oceanic whitetip shark (*Carcharhinus longimanus*), blue shark (*Prionace glauca*), and bull shark (*C. leucas*).

On April 18, 1935, a tiger shark measuring fourteen feet, six inches, was caught off Maroubra Point, New South Wales, Australia. It had become tangled in the setlines of commercial fishermen while it was feeding on a smaller shark that had been hooked. The animal was taken to the Coogee Aquarium in Sydney, where it was placed on exhibit. The huge shark, estimated to weigh 1,600 pounds, did not eat for a week, but swam incessantly around the pool. On April 25, it began to swim more actively; it flayed the water with its tail and vomited up several objects. According to the *Sydney Morning Herald* of April 26, the disgorged objects included, "pieces of flesh from another shark, a partly digested mutton-bird, a number of bones, and a human arm."

The arm, which had "a piece of kellick rope tied around the wrist" and a tattoo of two boxers on the shoulder, was taken to the coroner's office for examination. Australia's leading shark

Zane Grey poses with a tiger shark he caught in New Zealand. As tiger sharks get older, they lose their stripes.

OPPOSITE *Tiger sharks are considered among the most dangerous of all large sharks.*

authorities were called in, including Victor Coppleson, a surgeon with a particular interest in shark attacks; David G. Stead, an authority on sharks (whose extraordinary account of a "great, pale shark" appears "on page 22), and Gilbert P. Whitley, curator of fish at the Australian National Museum. They all agreed that the arm had been severed with a knife and not bitten off by the shark. Even though the shark was declared innocent of any crime, it was killed and butchered. No other human remains were found.

From the fingerprints and the tattoo, the arm was identified as belonging to one James Smith, a "billiard marker" from Gladesville, near Sydney. An extremely complicated investigation followed, with hints of multiple murders, drug traffic, dismembered bodies in trunks, and other sensational implications. The case, known as the "Shark Arm Murder," was never solved. The Australian Supreme Court, citing an English case from 1276, ruled that a single limb could not be considered a murder victim, and that without a corpus delicti, there was no murder. As far as the law was concerned, James Smith was still alive, even though his left arm had been swallowed by a shark.

Among the items that have been removed, at one time or another, from the stomachs of tiger sharks are boat cushions, rats, tin cans, turtles, the head of a crocodile, driftwood, seals, the hind leg of a sheep, conch shells, a tom-tom, horseshoe crabs, an unopened can of salmon, a wallet, a two-pound coil of copper wire, small sharks and other fish, nuts and bolts, lobsters, and lumps of coal. From this extensive catalog, it seems reasonable to assume that a tiger shark will eat virtually anything it finds in its waters, including people. (In certain parts of the world, especially the islands of the Caribbean, the tiger is the most feared of all sharks. The International Shark Attack File shows twenty-seven attacks definitely attributable to *Galeocerdo cuvieri*, and they have occurred all over the world, from Australia to Florida.)

On December 13, 1958, Billy Weaver, the son of a prominent Honolulu restaurant owner, was attacked and killed while surfing on an air mattress off Lanikai, on the east coast of Oahu. Even after the attack, the shark "was still cruising in plain sight nearby," and within the next few days, two tiger sharks, eleven and twelve feet in length, were caught in the immediate area. A great public outcry followed this gruesome incident, and in April 1959 the "Billy Weaver Shark Control Program" was started. Using three units of twenty-four-hook longline gear, 595 sharks were caught in inshore Oahu waters during the remainder of 1959, of which 71 (12 percent) were tigers. (For comparison, in the years 1964 to 1972, only 2 percent of the thousands of sharks caught in the nets used to mesh South African beaches were tigers.) In a dedicated campaign to rid Hawaii's waters of "dangerous" sharks, some 4,500 were killed under state auspices from 1959 to 1976, but no decrease in the number of attacks was recorded.

In his *Sharks and Survival* (1963), Jack Randall wrote, "If the identity of every shark attacking man in the tropical Atlantic were known, the tiger shark might well be responsible for more of them than any other species." The tiger shark is properly known as *Galeocerdo cuvier*; the generic name *Galeocerdo* means "cunning" or "weasel," and *cuvier* is the last name of the great nineteenth-century French naturalist Baron Georges Léopold Cuvier, the founder of comparative anatomy and vertebrate paleontology. The "tiger" part of the shark's common name does not come from the ferocity of the shark (although it probably could have), but rather from the fact that younger specimens have a strong pattern of stripes and blotches on their backs. The stripes usually fade with maturity, leaving the adult animal a dusky ocher above and lighter below, with only a faint hint of its juvenile pattern.

But even without stripes, this shark is particularly easy to identify. It has a very broad head that is almost square when viewed from above. Its nostrils, located near the front of the short snout, are quite pronounced, and its teeth, should you get close enough to examine them, are unique. They are sharp-pointed and serrated like those of many other species, but they are sharply notched on the side that faces away from the median line of the head, giving them an unmistakable cockscomb shape. As a further means of identification, the tiger shark has an upper tail lobe that is unusually long and pointed.

The largest of the charcharhinids, this species is found in all tropical and semitropical seas, except the Mediterranean. They prefer murky waters in coastal areas and are commonly found in estuaries, harbors, or inlets, where runoff may attract prey items. The largest specimen on record, taken off Cuba, weighed more than a ton. The current rod-and-reel record weighed 1,780 pounds and was caught in 1964 from the pier at Cherry Grove, South Carolina. This is the largest game fish caught on rod and reel in the Western Hemisphere.

OCEANIC WHITETIP SHARK

In *The Shark: Splendid Savage of the Sea* (1970), Jacques Cousteau gave us this description of the oceanic whitetip:

> While the brute strength of other sharks is tempered by their beauty and their elegance of form and movement, this species is absolutely hideous. His yellow-brown color is not uniform, but streaked with irregular markings like a bad job of military camouflage. His body is rounder than that of other sharks and the extremities of his enormous pectoral fins and his rounded dorsal fin look as if they had been dyed a dirty gray. He swims in a jerky, irregular manner, swinging his shortened, broad snout from side to side. His tiny eyes are hard and cruel-looking.

Cousteau calls it the "lord of the long hands" and "the most dangerous of all sharks." In the same book, he refers to the great white shark as the most fearsome looking, but accords the distinction of most dangerous to the oceanic whitetip, *Carcharhinus longimanus*.

Although it is one of the most abundant of the offshore sharks, very little is known of the habits of the oceanic whitetip shark. Because of the rapidity with which large numbers of these sharks congregate at the scene of a midocean disaster, the population of these sharks has been estimated to be extremely high. Thomas Lineaweaver and Richard Backus indicate that it is "extraordinarily abundant, perhaps the most abundant large animal, large being over 100 pounds, on the face of the earth." It is one of the few carcharhinids that can be easily differentiated from the others, thanks to the characteristics that give the shark its common and scientific names—the coloration of its fins and the length of its pectorals. The broadly rounded first dorsal fin, the second dorsal fin, and the upper lobe of the tail fin are tipped with white, and the other fins, such as the pectorals, often show this same coloration in mature whitetips. *Longimanus* means "long hands," and refers to the length of the pectoral fins. These extremely long fins are broad at the base and not as gracefully curved as those of the blue shark.

Jacques Cousteau was one of the inventors of the Aqua-Lung, and as one of the first men to use an artificial breathing apparatus in the open ocean, he was among the first people to swim with sharks of any kind. Much useful information has been gathered from his adventures, including data on sharks. In *The Silent World*, which was published in 1953, and was, therefore, one of the first popular books to deal with men and sharks in the water together, Cousteau tells of his first encounter with a whitetip shark. While diving off the Cape Verde Islands in the African Atlantic, "we saw a shark of a species we had never before seen. He was impressively neat, light gray, sleek, a real collector's item.... I tried to identify the species. The tail was quite asymmetrical, with an unusually long top, or heterocercal caudal fin. He had huge pectorals, and the dorsal fin was rounded with a white patch on it. In outline and marking he resembled no shark we had seen or studied."[†] For the sake of the camera, the divers toyed with this "collector's item" by pulling its tail, not knowing what sort of shark it was or how dangerous it might be.

In the 1970 book from which the opening quotation in this

[†] It is interesting to note that, over the years, Cousteau's opinion of this species changed from "neat" and "sleek" to "hideous," and his description of its color went from "light gray" to "yellow-brown ... a bad job of military camouflage."

The scientific name of the oceanic whitetip—Carcharhinus longimanus—refers to its long pectoral fins.

section is taken, Philippe Cousteau realizes that the shark they had come upon years earlier was "the great longimanus, well known to my father and all of us," and Jacques Cousteau himself calls that experience "a misadventure which I would judge very severely today."

The behavior of the whitetip has been variously described as indifferent, lackadaisical, and lethargic, but fortunately most humans do not have to test the validity of these observations. Its size and abundance would make it extremely dangerous to humans, if only they swam where *C. longimanus* swims. However,

this shark is definitely an inhabitant of the open ocean; it almost never comes close to shore. Henry Bigelow and William C. Schroeder did not find "a single report of [a shark] caught from the beach or taken in a pound net anywhere along the coast of the United States that could be referred with certainty to this particular species." We are probably safe, then, from being attacked while swimming or diving, but shipwrecks and airplane crashes in the ocean present a different picture altogether. In its home territory, *C. longimanus* has been shown to be aggressive, determined, and anything but lackadaisical. In its open-water domain it is abundant, large (estimates of its maximum length go as high as 13 feet, but the largest measured specimens have been no more than 10.5 feet), and almost never frightened. Stewart Springer (quoted by Lineaweaver and Backus) has described the dogged persistence of this shark: "I do not know of anything except a beaker of formalin poured down the gullet that elicits a very strong reaction. They continue a slow and persistent attack in spite of nonmortal bullet holes." Springer also described an incident aboard the research vessel *Oregon*, in which cherry bombs thrown into the water in the presence of feeding whitetips had no effect on them—except when a bomb was swallowed by one of the sharks and it exploded in the shark's mouth. With smoke and bits of flesh streaming from its gills, the shark moved off rapidly. Springer has observed that whitetips are dominant over other species of sharks, even when they are the same size.

In fewer than fifty years, the oceanic whitetip has fallen from its pedestal as the most numerous large animal in the world, and it has now aquired a new designation: endangered species. Given that it inhabits almost all the world's oceans in the temperate zone, this decline in numbers is especially troubling. As a blue-water shark, it is targeted by illegal fishing fleets, which seek out sharks of all kinds for the lucrative trade in fins for shark-fin soup. In the process known as "finning," the sharks are caught, their dorsal and pectoral fins are cut off, and the living, finless shark is then thrown back into the ocean to die. Shark-fin soup may sell for $100-a-bowl in restaurants in China, Singapore, Hong Kong, and other Asian locales. Many shark fisheries around the world—Mexico, for example—are in business largely to supply fins to this market. In some parts of the world, finning is so widespread that the local populations of sharks have become

endangered. In 1991, 2,289 sharks were landed in Honolulu. By 1998, the number had leapt to 60,857 (a 2,500 percent increase), and of that total, 99 percent was for fins. The large size of its fins and its offshore habitat, far from the prying eyes of fisheries regulators, has been the death knell for the global population of oceanic whitetips. The International Union for the Conservation of Nature (IUCN) currently lists the species as "near threatened."

In the Gulf of Mexico, where oceanic whitetips were once so common that they were considered a nuisance to fishermen, they are now virtually extinct. Elsewhere in the world's ocean, long-lining for these and other large predatory fish has resulted in a catastrophic decline: More than 90 percent of all the sharks, tuna, billfish, cod, and groupers are gone, and fishermen are now working on the remaining 10 percent. In a 2003 study titled "Collapse and Conservation of Shark Populations in the Northwest Atlantic," it is noted that only the threshers, with an overall decline of 80 percent, are in worse shape than the oceanic whitetips. *Carcharhinus longimanus*, the lord of the long hands, has declined by 70 percent.

BLUE SHARK

In *Moby-Dick* (1851), sharks feed on the carcass of a sperm whale that is swimming alongside the whaleship *Pequod*. Herman Melville describes the actions of two seamen who beat the sharks in an attempt to keep them away from the whale:

> No small excitement was created among the sharks, for immediately upon suspending the cutting stages over the side, and suspending three lanterns so that they cast long gleams of light over the turbid sea, these two mariners, darting their long whaling-spades, kept up an incessant murdering of the sharks by striking the keen steel deep into their skulls, seemingly their only vital part. But in the foamy confusion of their mixed and struggling hosts, the marksmen could not always hit their mark; and this brought new revelations of the incredible ferocity of the foe. They viciously snapped, not only at each other's disembowelments, but like flexible bows, bent round and bit their own.

The sharks in this episode are not identified by species, but the blue shark, *Prionace glauca*, is infamous for its ravenous feeding on harpooned whales. In fact, the Australians call this shark the "blue whaler" for just this reason, and blues were the predominant species found feeding on the whale carcass when Peter Gimbel, Stan Waterman, and Ron and Valerie Taylor made their night dives off the whaling grounds of Durban during the filming of *Blue Water, White Death* (1971).

The passage from Melville is also significant beause it describes so well the "feeding frenzy" that sharks will fall into in the presence of large amounts of food, such as a whale, plentiful fish, or offal, and a large enough number of competing sharks. As individuals, blues are no more susceptible to this mob feeding than any other species of shark, but blues are unusually plentiful and found in higher concentrations than most other species, so the possibilities of mass feedings are correspondingly higher.

At the Bay Shore Mako Tournament, held every summer on Long Island, blues are caught almost ten times more often than all other species combined. (In 1965, a total of 918 sharks were caught, and only 7 were not blues.) If you are fishing or diving off Long Island and you see a shark, chances are that it is a blue. In Peter Gimbel's first shark film, *In the World of Sharks*, the only sharks he saw besides blues while making the film (shot off the coast of Montauk, using Frank Mundus's *Cricket II* and a prototype shark cage—which, surprisingly, Gimbel stayed outside of for much of the filming) were one mako and one small tiger shark. Taking advantage of the fact that the abudance of blues carries over from the Atlantic to the Pacific coast, in California, Scott Johnson and Don Nelson do most of their work with blue sharks as their subjects. (Interestingly enough, the blue shark in the Pacific, although it is the same species as the Atlantic version, never gets much bigger than six feet in length.) Jack Casey's shark-tagging program, based at the Narragansett Laboratory of the National Marine Fisheries Service in Rhode Island, although nominally involved with all species, is also primarily concerned with the tagging of blue sharks.

The bluedog or great blue shark, to use some of its other vernacular names, is a lithe, graceful animal, proportionally slimmer than any other carcharhinid. Although there have been reports of blues reaching twenty feet, the longest on record is twelve feet seven inches, and the International Game Fish Association all-tackle record is for a shark eleven feet six inches long. This fish, caught in 1960 off Rockport, Massachusetts, weighed 410 pounds. (Just for comparison, an eleven-foot eight-inch mako weighed 854 pounds, and the mako is not regarded as a particularly heavy-bodied shark.) Fishing for blue sharks is not the most exciting sport in the world—one tends to chum them up to the boat and then "hand-feed" them the bait—but it is hard work. They are not showy fighters, but they are usually determined not to be brought in, and the power of a large blue shark is quickly felt in the angler's back and shoulders.

OPPOSITE *True to its name, the blue shark is a deep ultramarine above and white below.*

The blue shark is long in almost all respects: long snout, long tail, long body, and especially long, curved pectoral fins. These thin, flexible fins contribute to the blue shark's extraordinary maneuverability in the water. Only the blue's teeth cannot be considered long by shark-teeth standards, but they are particularly sharp and numerous—a blue shark can take a twenty-pound bite out of the carcass of a whale, a bite that looks as if it were made with a giant ice cream scoop.

Not surprisingly, the blue shark is named for its color, but the color itself is surprising—it is a rich ultramarine (a fine name for the color of a shark, I think) that changes to a silvery white beneath. As with many other fish, the color fades quickly with death, and blue sharks brought to the dock appear a drab slate or smoky gray.

The blue shark is not usually considered dangerous, but it has the size and the equipment to be taken seriously. There are a number of people who have dived with blues with trepidation and no accidents, but the International Shark Attack File lists eight unprovoked attacks on people, and three attacks on boats. Of course, the attacks where the species was not identified are not listed in the blue shark's column—so it may in fact have more attacks to its credit.

None of the records or files kept on shark attacks have indicated the species of sharks attracted to the scene of major shipwrecks or air disasters, where it is possible to attribute many of the deaths and injuries to the "feeding frenzy." For example, in 1942, when the troop-carrier *Nova Scotia* was torpedoed off the coast of South Africa, there were more than one thousand persons aboard, many of whom were injured in the initial explosions, but many more of whom were maimed or killed by the sharks that were attracted to the scene of the disaster. When rescue vessels arrived the next morning, they found many of the victims with limbs bitten off, clinging to bits of the wreckage. Many of the sharks in those waters were blues.

One of the most graceful of sharks, the blue shark (Prionace glauca) *can reach a maximum length of twelve feet.*

BULL SHARK

IN THE NOVEL *JAWS*, PETER BENCHLEY makes reference to a series of grisly shark attacks that occurred off New Jersey during the summer of 1916. On July 1, while playing in the surf some fifteen yards from shore in Beach Haven, Charles Vansant was bitten on the left thigh. His companions dragged him to shore and applied a tourniquet to his wound, but he had lost so much blood that he died. Five days later, at a resort some forty-five miles north of Beach Haven, Charles Bruder was killed by a shark that bit off both of his feet. Then eleven-year-old Lester Stillwell was the victim of another fatal strike at Matawan Creek on July 11, and when Stanley Fisher dove in to rescue Stillwell, he too was attacked, and later died on the operating table. The last event in this gruesome series also occurred on July 12 in Matawan Creek, when young Joseph Dunn was bitten on the left leg. Although his leg was severely lacerated, he made a full recovery.

Because the attacks ceased after a fisherman named Michael Schleisser caught a seven-foot six-inch white shark in Raritan Bay on July 14, people seemed ready to regard this shark as the perpetrator. It was believed that all the assaults had been committed by a single "rogue" white shark; in fact, *Jaws* is predicated on the same reasoning. But there are certain inconsistencies in this theory. First of all, the attacks took place over great distances—the first was ninety miles from the last—and there is no basis for the assumption that a single shark would travel so far just to bite people. (In none of the attacks was any significant amount of tissue removed, indicating that the shark was probably not feeding.) Second, the three attacks in Matawan Creek occurred in freshwater, where white sharks are not known to enter. And finally, the "rogue shark" theory, originally introduced by Australian surgeon Victor Coppleson, has been completely repudiated. Sharks simply do not alter their diet after tasting human flesh, and even more important, sharks are probably not interested in eating people.

We still do not have an explanation for why shark attacks occur, but recent studies suggest that sharks may be protecting their territory or even mistaking swimmers or surfers for seals. From the shark's vantage point, a surfer on a short surfboard, arms and legs extended, probably looks a lot like a sea lion. Sharks are not great intellectuals, and since they have been feeding on things that look like seals for millions of years, they are, presumably, programmed to attack anything that resembles one. In New Jersey, people have been swimming recreationally for only about 150 years, so the sharks cannot be blamed for not adjusting their habits quickly enough. Prior to the invention of swimming, diving, and surfing, anything in the shark's domain was fair game.

A much more likely culprit in the 1916 attacks is the bull shark (*Carcharhinus leucas*), which is common off the New Jersey coasts and regularly enters freshwater (one was found one thousand miles up the Mississippi River). Instead of a single "rogue shark," we can substitute several bull sharks. Says shark expert Leonard Compagno: "It would not surprise the writer if this species turned out to be the most dangerous living shark because of its large size, massive jaws, and proportionately very large teeth, abundance in the tropics . . . indiscriminate appetite and propensity to take largish prey, and close proximity to human activities in both fresh and salt water." During July 1916, there were many more "human activities" taking place in the Jersey surf, for the East Coast was in the grip of a massive heat wave. It follows, then, that with so many more potential victims in the water, there just might be an increase in the number of shark attacks. The bull shark may be even more dangerous to humans than the white, but with its mouse gray coloring and smaller size (the maximum length for a bull shark is ten feet; for a white shark, more than twenty—and the white shark can reach a weight of two tons, compared with a four-hundred-pound bull), it looks comparatively nondescript next to the fabled man-eater.

OPPOSITE *Because of its inclination to enter fresh water rivers, the bull shark* (Carcharhinus leucas) *might be the most dangerous shark of all.*

GREY NURSE *or* SAND TIGER SHARK

THE SAND TIGERS (ODONTASPIDS) are the embodiment of all that is confusing, contradictory, and controversial in the study of sharks. Almost everything about them has been in dispute at one time or another, from their nature to their very name. For a while, the odontaspids were known as the Carchariidae. In 1948, Bigelow and Schroeder were content to use this name (in their definitive *Fishes of the Western North Atlantic*), but then the name *Odontaspis* (which means "snaketooth") was adopted. Not that it was not used before—in 1838, the zoologist Louis Agassiz suggested it—but as these sharks swam silently in the world's shallow offshore waters, their names were changed and changed again. As of now they are the family Odontaspidae, and their generic name is *Carcharias*.

At one time in the not so distant past, these sharks were neatly divided into several geographically segregated species, each with its own common name. In the western North Atlantic, for example, there was the sand tiger shark; in South African waters it was the ragged-tooth; and Australian waters were home to the grey nurse shark. Nothing is more confusing to nonscientists than different common names, which is the reason for scientific names in the first place. When somebody writes (or says) "*Carcharias taurus*," everyone—that is, everyone who cares about biological accuracy—knows what kind of shark they are talking about, whether they speak Hindi, Swedish, or Swahili. It

is now accepted that all of these sharks, whether found in the waters of Australia, South Africa, South America, Japan, India, or China, are members of the same species, *Carcharias taurus*. (Another problem with the popular nomenclature is that the "sand tiger" is not related to the tiger shark *Galeocerdo cuvier*, and the "grey nurse" is not related to the nurse shark, *Ginglymostoma cirratum*.)

All odontaspids are grayish brown above, lighter below, and they often have a series of irregular dark spots on their flanks. They have a pointed, slightly upturned snout, and teeth that are always erect and decidedly "fanglike." The fins are heavy and fleshy, often tipped with black on the posterior margins. The first dorsal is situated fairly far back (it originates behind the posterior margins of the pectorals), and it is close to the second dorsal, which is almost as large as the first. The base of the tail is stocky, and its movement, at least in aquarium specimens, is slow and steady. In the wild, however, they must be capable of swift rushes, since they feed on such speedsters as bluefish and bonito. They are omnivorous, and examination of their stomach contents has shown that they feed on many other fish, including slow swimmers and bottom dwellers, and occasionally even crabs. Bigelow and Schroeder maintain "there is no reason to suppose that this species ever attacks large prey."

Odontaspids are ovoviviparous (until they hatch, their eggs

remain in the mother's body), which is the common method of parturition in most sharks, but the embryos are also *oviphagous* ("egg-eating"), which is uncommon in any creature. Two embryos develop in the uterus, one in each side. Each embryo then consumes the eggs as they come down the oviduct, accounting for their large size at birth (about three feet). Sand tiger embryos can be dangerous before they are born, as can be attested to by Stewart Springer, who was bitten by an unborn specimen while he was examining a gravid female. Odontaspids have developed a peculiar habit in aquariums. They rise to the top of the tank to gulp a mouthful of air, which, retained in the stomach, acts as sort of a swim bladder. It is not known if they do this in their natural habitat, and no other species is known to do it, in the sea or in captivity.

These sharks are very sharky in appearance, with staring yellow eyes and a mouthful of the wickedest-looking teeth in sharkdom. They reach a maximum length of about ten feet in the Atlantic, but larger ones have been reported in other locations. Because this species is unaggressive and fairly easy to catch, it is often seen as an aquarium specimen. One adult specimen in the Durban aquarium was never known to accept the cut-up fish that the other sharks ate, but "presumably kept her portly proportions by making a meal of the smaller sharks around her at night." As long as I can remember, there have been sand tigers in evidence at the New York Aquarium at Coney Island, and they were kept at the earlier New York Aquarium at Battery Park long before that. At the Taronga Park Aquarium in Sydney, a female grey nurse lived for six years in a sixty- by forty-foot pool. She ate 170 to 200 pounds of fish per year, averaging about 50 pounds a month from February to April, but only 3 to 4 pounds a month from May to August, the Australian winter. In 1958, at Marine Studios in Florida, the first sand tiger was born in captivity.

Despite its fierce appearance, the sand tiger is considered harmless in American waters. Only one attack has been recorded, and this seems to have been provoked. Ranging further afield in the literature, we discover that it had a totally different reputation in other parts of the world. For instance, in 1963, J. L. B. Smith, an authority on the fish of South Africa, described it this way:

A cunning and quiet scavenger which creeps along the bottom towards the shore, and when stationary in even only 4 ft. of water,

the largest specimen is hardly visible against a sandy bottom. If an unwary bather approaches within reach there is a savage rush, and usually another fatality. Even if the victim escapes, the terrible teeth cause fearful lacerations. Probably most shallow water attacks in South Africa are due to this Shark which also penetrates far up estuaries. The jaws of a 10 ft. specimen would easily sever a human head or thigh, those of the largest would easily cut a man in half.

Most of this is wrong, as is Smith's assertion that it can reach a length of twenty feet. In the first of his Investigational Reports on shark attacks in South African waters, David Davies, of the Oceanographic Research Institute at Durban, attributed an attack on a swimmer to a ragged-tooth, but he later revised the attribution to the bull or Zambezi shark, *Carcharhinus leucas*. The South African sharks are far from the "cunning" man-eaters of Smith's description. At the Durban aquarium in 1966, a program of hand-feeding two small ragged-tooths was inaugurated, in an attempt to discover what they preferred in the way of food. The sharks, named Porgy and Bess, preferred stockfish to tuna, would not eat whale meat or beef, and never bit the hand that fed them.

In Australia, the reputation of the grey nurse varies greatly, depending on the source. Victor Coppleson in *Shark Attack* includes this species in the category of sharks to be "regarded with suspicion, or which have had attacks attributed to them." Ben Cropp, a shark-killer whose books detail his abilities to spear, poison, stab, explode, shoot, and otherwise dispatch all sorts of sharks, spent a great deal of time in pursuit of grey nurse sharks, because they were "placid ... and easy to spear." Valerie Taylor, who, with her husband, Ron, accompanied Cropp on some of the early shark killing and filming expeditions, wrote this to me in a letter:

It has been my experience that the Grey Nurse is a harmless shark, as far as attacking man is concerned. It will not attack man. This does not mean it will not defend itself. I am sick to death of skindivers saying how they were attacked by a Grey Nurse after they had speared it. In every case the poor creature was trying to escape and the diver got in the way.

J. L. B. Smith was wrong and Valerie was right. Smith was the discoverer of the coelacanth, and South Africa's most famous ichthyologist, so people were more than willing to believe his pronouncements—even when he was making them up. The shark was a victim of its fearsome appearance; it looks as if it ought to be dangerous, and therefore people were more than willing to consider it so. The misrepresentation of this completely harmless shark encouraged brave divers to shoot them with spearguns, to show that they could conquer such a dangerous creature. It was partially this misdirected machismo that led to the grey nurse's downfall—at least in Australia. Some were caught commercially

for their fins, but the grey nurse's malevolent visage brought many people into its habitat, to do battle with the "man-eater." So many of these sharks were killed that by 2002, the Australian government listed the species as endangered. It is illegal in New South Wales and Queensland waters to catch a grey nurse shark, either from a boat or while diving. If a man is caught with a grey nurse, the fines can run as high as $220,000.

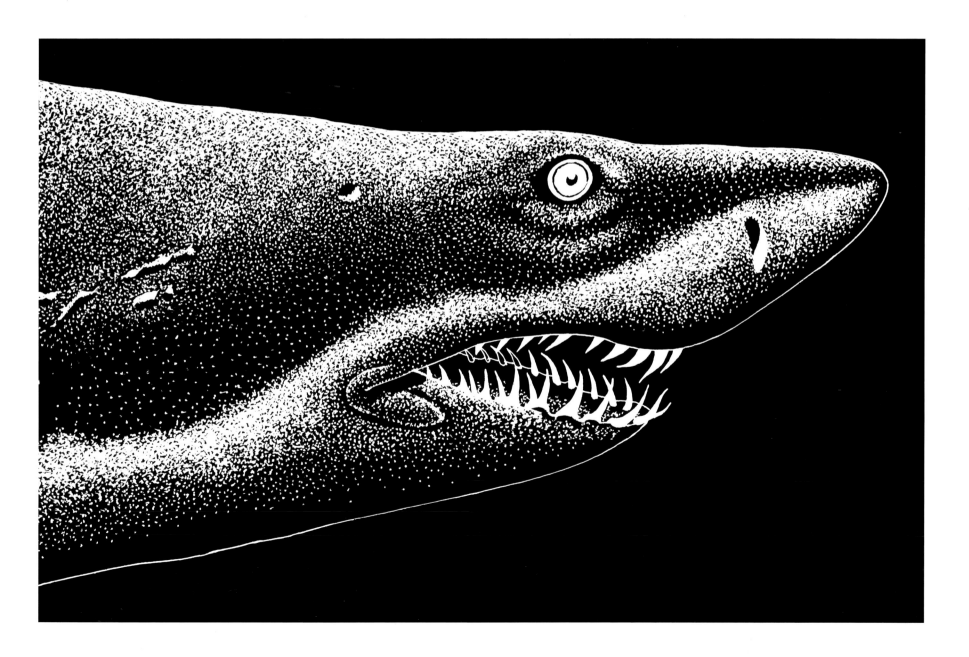

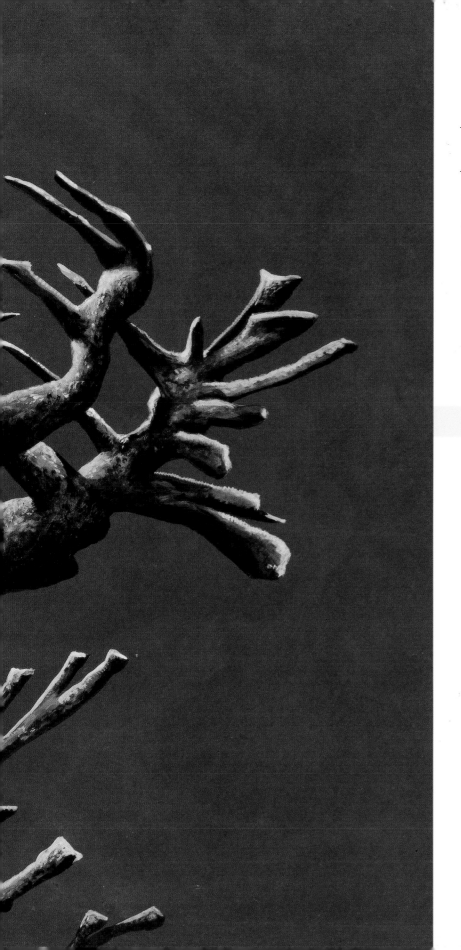

HAMMERHEAD SHARK

THE HAMMERHEADS (THERE ARE nine nominal species in the genus *Sphyrna*) are probably the strangest looking of all sharks. There are species of sharks with spots, ridges, spines, stripes, and occasionally a long nose or tail, but nothing in the shark world can match the hammerheads for weirdness. All nine species have greatly elongated and flattened lobes on the head, on which the eyes and nostrils are located. One of the criteria used to differentiate the nine species is the shape and size of these lobes, which are responsible for the genus's vernacular name. The Roman poet Oppian called them "balance fish," and others have called them shovelhead, scoophead, bonnethead, and *cornuda* ("horned" in Spanish).

Hammerheads are brownish to grayish above and lighter below, like the carcharhinids, which they closely resemble in general body shape. Species can be told apart by detailed measurements of the fins, body, and teeth. The smallest of the hammerheads, *Sphyrna tiburo*, rarely exceeds five feet in length. It does not have a proper "hammer," but a flattened, rounded head, shaped rather like a shovel. For some reason, this fish has entered the language as "bonnethead." Bonnetheads are harmless, gregarious sharks, often found in small schools of eight to fifteen individuals. They inhabit the shallow waters of bays and estuaries in the Western Hemisphere, from New England to Brazil.

S. *mokarran* is the largest of the genus, reported to reach a length of twenty feet. One of the distinguishing characteristics of the great hammerhead is its exceptionally tall dorsal fin. Studying the larger hammerheads has proved to be far more difficult than studying the smaller ones, for they are renowned for their fragility and thus are almost never seen in captivity. In 1974, a large female (eleven feet, 417 pounds) of the species survived long enough at Marineland in Florida to give birth to four live pups in an exhibition tank, but she died within an hour (probably as a result of the struggle to bring her in). The pups lasted only a couple of days. When the female was autopsied, she was found to contain another twenty-four pups. Observers did note that the "hammer" and fins of the four viable pups were quite flexible at birth, allowing passage through the cloaca of the female. (Gravid female hammerheads are caught rather frequently, and the inclusion of a macabre picture of a mother lying dead beside her thirty or forty babies is not uncommon in books about sharks or books about fishing.)

Thanks to their obvious difference in appearance from other large sharks, the hammerheads that have been authoritatively implicated in shark attacks have not been confused with any other sharks. One of the most celebrated cases of an interaction between a hammerhead and a man took place in 1805, when Joshua Terry of Riverhead, Long Island, netted three large hammerheads. The largest specimen was shown to contain "many detached parts of a man," as well as some articles of clothing, but it was not known if the man had been dead before being ingested. There are a number of cases in the International Shark Attack File of unprovoked attacks on boats and swimmers by hammerheads.

The great hammerhead is found throughout the tropical and subtropical waters of the world, but some records conflate two similar species, S. *zygaena* and S. *lewini*, which are both fairly large. S. *mokarran* is best recognized by the nearly flat leading edge of its "T"-shaped head; in this species, the head is most nearly rectangular. S. *lewini*, sometimes known as the "scalloped" hammerhead, has a more rounded head, and S. *zygaena* (from the Greek *zygon* for "yoke") has pronounced indentations on the front of the head at the location of the nostrils. In all Sphyrnidae, the nostrils are located on the front edge of the "hammer," which presumably gives the genus an olfactory advantage over other sharks, whose nostrils are closer together and located under the overhanging snout.

Ever since people have been writing about hammerheads, there has been speculation as to the "purpose" of their strange lobes. Among the theories that have been suggested are the following: They give the shark added lift or help in diving, like a hydroplane; they increase the shark's maneuverability, possibly by decreasing the turning radius; they enable the shark to "triangulate" and better locate prey, by separating the eyes and nostrils; and even that the grotesque shape of the head serves to frighten rival predators away. Only one author, Paul Budker, has suggested that the lobes might also be a detriment: "In a tussle with a Tiger Shark or a White Shark, the adversary could easily inflict great damage with its jaws on these vulnerable parts." The hammerheads are the most recently evolved sharks, and so we might be seeing an evolutionary experiment at this moment. It is rather difficult to assign the concept of "detrimental development" to an animal that we have always thought of as being so perfectly evolved, but overspecialization is also thought to be one of the major causes of extinction.

All of the theories about the function of the lobes may be true to a certain extent; such complex and unique structures probably serve more than one purpose. There is a theory that takes into account not only the hydrodynamic properties of the lobes, but their physical and electrical capabilities as well. All sharks have a series of subcutaneous pit organs on the underside of the snout called the ampullae of Lorenzini, which are sensitive to chemical, physical, and thermal changes in the water. Early experiments showed that certain sharks were sensitive to weak electrical fields. Eventually, researchers concluded that, in addition to their other functions, the ampullae of Lorenzini were electroreceptors. In fact, sharks and rays possess the greatest degree of electrical sensitivity in the animal kingdom. In tests with rays and catsharks, for example, it was shown that these groups are able to use this electrical sensitivity to detect prey that is buried in the sand. In any event, the head of a sphyrnid is ideally designed to present the largest possible number of ampullae to the floor of the ocean, since the head is very much flattened and has a large surface area. The shark swims close to the bottom, swinging its head in a "minesweeper" action, covering much more territory than a shark with an ordinary head would. Therefore,

A giant hammerhead turns to face the photographer, showing the strangest visage in the animal kingdom.

it stands a much better chance of detecting the presence of prey buried in the sand. (The pectoral fins of the hammerheads are proportionally small, and this seems to support the idea of this shark's needing to get as close to the bottom as possible.) Although hammerheads are known to be almost omnivorous, they seem to favor stingrays as a dietary staple. It is a rare hammerhead that does not have at least one stingray spine embedded in its jaw, and Perry Gilbert reported in 1966 on one large specimen that was found to have ninety-six barbs in its jaw, mouth, and head.

GOBLIN SHARK

THIS LITTLE-KNOWN, weird-looking pink shark, *Mitsukurina owstoni*, is believed to grow as long as eighteen feet, much of which consists of the upper lobe of its heterocercal tail (that is, one where the upper lobe is significantly longer than the lower, and characteristic of most sharks); a further contribution is made by the bizarre extension of its rostrum, or snout, a paddlelike blade that overhangs the protrusible jaws. When the first specimens were examined it was suggested that the goblin shark uses the blade to stir up sediment on the ocean floor in search of food, but recent examinations have shown that the rostrum—like the head lobes of the hammerhead—is rich in sensory receptors, enabling the shark to locate prey buried in the sand and in the dark, because it is believed to be a deepwater species. Goblin sharks hunt by sensing the presence of prey with these electrosensitive organs; once the prey is located, the shark suddenly thrusts its jaws forward, while using a tonguelike muscle to suck the victim into its sharp front teeth. Its awl-like teeth and protrusible jaws seem to indicate that it is a fish eater, but this is only a supposition as very little is known of its feeding habits (both attempts to keep goblin sharks alive in captivity failed within days). Its pink coloration, unique among sharks, is due to blood vessels underneath a semitransparent skin that bruises easily.

In the nineteenth century, the fossil remains of a Cretaceous sharklike vertebrate were found in Syrian chalk beds and elsewhere. It was classified as *Scapanorhynchus*, meaning "shovel-snout," because of its strange overhanging beak. Unlike the rostrum of a sawfish or the bill of a marlin or a swordfish, this strange protrusion seemed unrelated to the mouth; it is not an extension of the upper lip, but more like a greatly elongated nose or even a horn emanating from the forehead. The fossil shark had a proper set of jaws, independent of the strange protuberance. It was classified with other archaic sharks, and those who follow the doctrine of natural selection assumed that it had become extinct millions of years ago, to be replaced by more "successful" sharks.

The first specimen of the modern species was caught in the "Black Tide" (Kuroshio Current) off Yokohama, Japan, in 1897. Japanese fishermen called the 3.5–foot male *tenguzame*, which means "goblin shark." This odd-looking shark was brought to the attention of Dr. David Starr Jordan, a leading authority on the fish of Japan and, at the time, the president of Stanford University. Jordan believed that the shark was new to science, and since he could not place it in any known family, he created a new one for it. He named it *Mitsukurina owstoni*, after Professor Kakichi Mitsukuri, a Japanese ichthyologist, and Alan Owston, a natural history dealer from Yokohama. Jordan's designation was not destined to last, since upon publication, paleontologists were quick to notice that this "new species" was in fact a very old species; it was the same animal as the Cretaceous fossil shark *Scapanorhynchus*, thought to have been extinct for one hundred million years. By 1910, the necessary revision had been published, and the living and the fossil shark shared the same name, *Scapanorhynchus*. Since then, the name given to it by Jordan has been restored.

The goblin shark is extremely rare, found mostly in deep waters off Japan, but also in the environs of Australia, New Zealand, and South Africa, as well as near Portugal. And, in one strange instance, in the Indian Ocean, where the raising of a length of cable that had been at 4,500 feet revealed a goblin shark's tooth embedded in the wire covering. The shark is thought to have been feeding on some sort of animal life growing on the cable at that depth. Goblin sharks are occasionally encountered as fisheries' bycatch: As they stay near the sea bottom, they are usually caught via deep, bottom-set gillnets and longline fishing. In 2003, more than a hundred goblin sharks were caught off the northwest coast of Taiwan, an area in which they have previously not been found and where, reportedly, an earthquake had recently occurred. In January 2007, a four-foot-long goblin shark was caught alive in Tokyo Bay, and put on exhibit at the Tokyo Sea Life Park. It had been tangled in fishing nets that were deployed at a depth of about six hundred feet. Many people came to see this unusual creature, but it died within a few days.

Aptly named, the goblin shark (Mitsukurina owstoni) is one of the weirdest-looking of all sharks.

SIXGILL SHARK

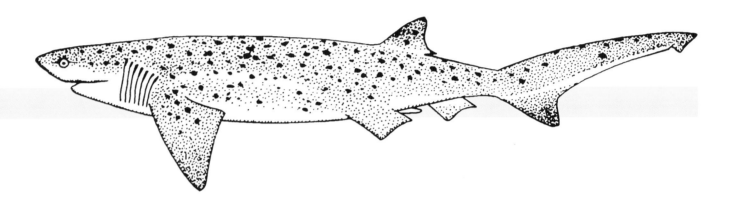

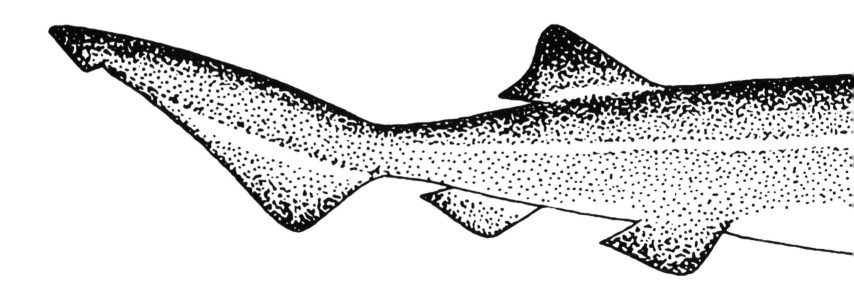

MOST LIVING SHARK SPECIES have five pairs of gills, but there are some with six and one species with seven. The sixgill and sevengill sharks are grouped together as Hexanchidae, derived from the Greek *hexa* meaning "six" and *ankos*, "gill." The teeth of the hexanchids are strikingly different in the upper and lower jaws. The upper teeth are similar to those of many other shark species, consisting of a central spire flanked by one or more smaller cusps. The lower teeth, however, are extraordinary, looking not like teeth at all, but like backward-pointing combs. The first cusp is the largest and the rest (in some species there are as many as ten subsidiary cusps) form a row decreasing in size toward the posterior portion of the tooth.

Hexanchus griseus is a temperate-water species found in the deeper waters of the Mediterranean (where it is fairly common), on both sides of the Atlantic, and in the Pacific. John Isaacs and Richard Schwarzlose of the Scripps Institute of Oceanography at La Jolla, California, obtained robotic-camera images of certain bottom-dwelling fish, including large sharks that frequent the deep ocean floor at depths down to 6,500 feet. In a spectacular photograph accompanying an article about these experiments in *Scientific American* in 1975, there is a "fifteen-foot shark" feeding at 2,400 feet in the eastern

Mediterranean. Because of its size, color, and location, the shark is almost certainly *H. griseus*, and this therefore is one of the few photographs ever taken of the sixgill shark in its native habitat.

The common name of *H. griseus* is the bluntnose sixgill, but it is also called the cow shark, mud shark, comb-toothed shark, and bulldog shark. Until 1969, it was thought to be the only species of sixgill shark in the genus *Hexanchus*. Then Stewart Springer and R. A. Wailer described a second species, *H. vitulus*, based on a specimen taken in the Bahamas. Since that time, a number of specimens thought to have been *H. griseus* have been identifiable as *H. vitulus*. *Vitulus* seems to be a warmer-water species, found off Florida, the Philippines, Madagascar, and the Kenyan coast south of Natal. The two species are differentiated primarily by the shape of their snouts, the number of rows of teeth in their jaws, the size of their eyes (hence the common name *H. vitulus*, bigeye sixgill), and their relative sizes. *H. griseus* is the larger of the two, reaching a length of fifteen feet and perhaps even more; *H. vitulus* rarely exceeds seven feet. With the exception of these morphological differences, the sharks are similar in biology and behavior. Both are deepwater species that may occasionally make excursions to the surface. They are dark-colored, described variously as "coffee-colored," "dark gray," or "mouse gray," and often there is no significant difference between the dorsal and the ventral coloration. They are ovoviviparous, and the number of embryos can range from 7 to 104 in the females examined.

In Lineaweaver and Backus's *Natural History of Sharks* (1986), there is an interesting story about *H. griseus* that "exemplifies how errors can be unwittingly propagated time and again." In 1846, Jonathan Couch reported a specimen that was "2 feet 6.5 inches." Shortly thereafter, mention was made of a specimen twenty-six feet five inches long, captured at Polperro, in Cornwall (the same location as Couch's specimen). This monstrous sixgill appears regularly in the literature, even though no specimen was ever taken after that one that even approached it in size. (It is cited in Bigelow and Schroeder, *Fishes of the Western North Atlantic* [1948], but with a disclaimer: "One of 26 feet 5 inches was reported from Cornwall many years ago, a giant of its kind *if its size was stated correctly.*") Lineaweaver and Backus suggest that the decimal point migrated, and 2 feet 6.5 inches was somehow converted to 26.5 inches and later (after Couch's death in 1870), by inadvertence or misinterpretation, turned into 26 feet 5 inches.

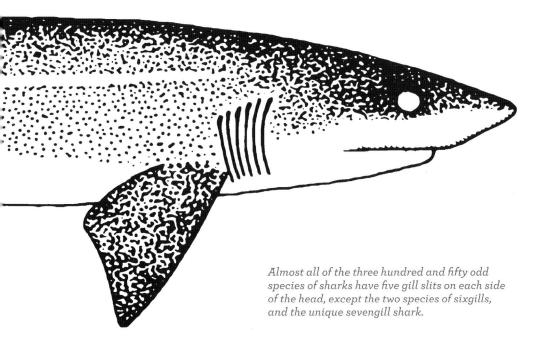

Almost all of the three hundred and fifty odd species of sharks have five gill slits on each side of the head, except the two species of sixgills, and the unique sevengill shark.

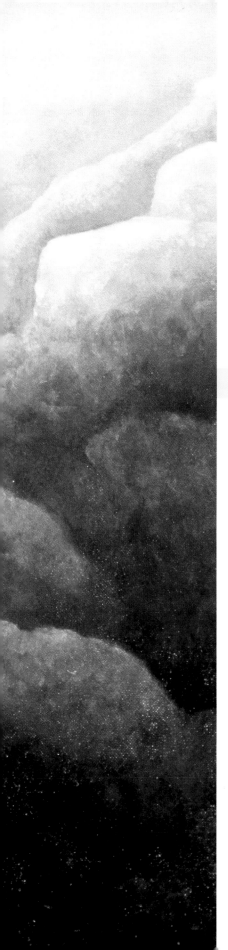

GREENLAND SHARK

THE GIGANTIC SHARK *Somniosus microcephalus* is known variously as the "Greenland shark," "sleeper shark," or "gurry shark." The "sleeper" appellation comes from its sluggish habits, and "gurry" is slang for the offal swept overboard after fishing or whaling operations, a reference to the shark's habit of hanging around docks or ships for scraps. At a known maximum length of twenty-three feet, this is one of the largest known sharks, period, and the largest of all deepwater fish. Greenland sharks are found in the colder waters of the higher North Atlantic latitudes, usually at depth, although they come closer to the surface in summer (one was filmed off Cape Hatteras, North Carolina, at a depth of 7,436 feet). It is believed that these sharks indeed feed mostly on carrion, although there has been little study of their habits; there are questionable records of individuals found with whole caribou in their stomachs. They are also known to feed on fish, which usually appear in their stomach contents with missing tails: Because *Somniosus* is often found with a parasitic copepod covering each eye, it has been speculated that the copepod's bioluminescence attracts the fish to the shark, which eats them headfirst. The Inuit fish for these sharks through holes in the ice, and although the flesh is poisonous when fresh, it can be eaten if it is dried or boiled several times. The Greenland shark is found in the northern reaches of the Atlantic, occasionally straying as far south as the Gulf of Maine. A smaller version, known as *S. rostrata*, inhabits the Mediterranean, and reaches a maximum length of four feet. A similar species, the Pacific sleeper shark (*S. pacificus*), is found from Japan to Puget Sound.

Long believed to inhabit the deep, icy waters of northern ocean basins, the Greenland shark has recently been seen in the frigid, murky waters of the St. Lawrence River in Quebec. In 2003, after tracking the enigmatic animal for five years, Chris Harvey-Clark and fellow diving enthusiast Jeffrey Gallant followed leads to Baie-Comeau, a small town about 250 miles northeast of Quebec City. There, the pair documented—for the first time under natural conditions—Greenland sharks reveling in shallow water. The Gulf of St. Lawrence, with a water temperature hovering around 36°F, had been a scuba-diving training ground for decades without any notable Greenland shark sightings. Interestingly, none of the sharks observed in this area have parasites on their eyes. "The sharks in the St. Lawrence have beautiful, crystal-clear eyes and are quite visual. As you swim by, their eyes swivel and follow you, which sets them apart from the population in the Arctic," says Harvey-Clark. "They probably don't see very well, but using a variety of other sensory modalities, they are very effective, stealthy predators and could take out an agile seal in zero visibility without alerting it."

The Greenland shark, named for its icy habitat, is one of the largest sharks, with a maximum length of twenty-three feet.

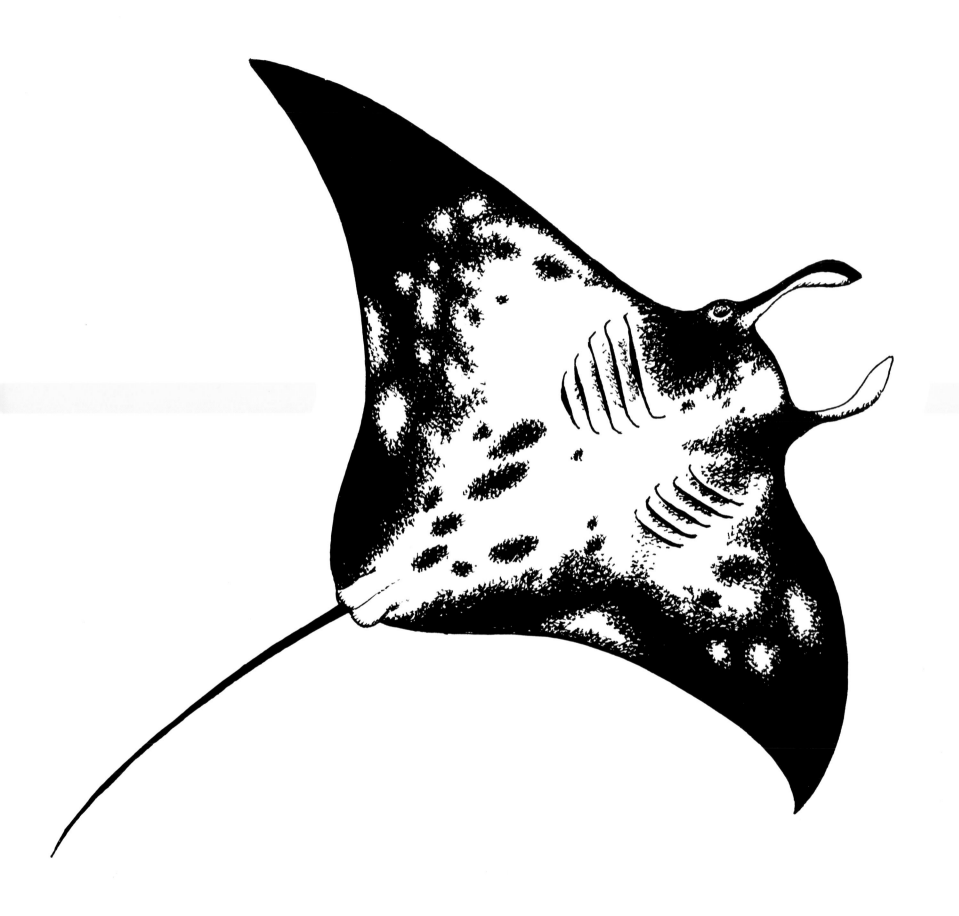

MANTA RAY

THERE ARE SEVERAL MARINE CREATURES large enough to have frightened uneducated observers, but as we learned more about them, they turned out not to be monsters after all. One animal was initially perceived as a true terror of the deep, but turned out to be a harmless, graceful, gentle giant, now eagerly sought by scuba divers for a free ride on its broad back. It is the manta ray, the largest of all rays; with its pointed wings, whiplike tail, strange-looking cephalic "horns," and a remarkable propensity to throw itself out of the water, it was known for years as "devilfish."

The largest of all rays are the Atlantic manta (*Manta birostris*) and the Pacific manta (*M. hamiltoni*), both of which can have wingspans of twenty feet and weigh more than a ton and a half. They swim—usually near the surface, where they feed on plankton—by slowly flapping their powerful pectoral wings. Of all the skates and rays, mantas are truly creatures of the surface—and beyond. A spectacular sight is a one-ton manta, black on the dorsal surface and white on the ventral, launching itself completely out of the water, and reentering with a thunderous splash. The reason for these prodigious leaps is unknown.

Because of their imposing size and strength, rays were not always recognized as harmless to anything but plankton, and they were feared and reviled by the people who first saw them. In 1919, *National Geographic* ran an article titled "Devil-fishing in the Gulf Stream" by John Oliver La Gorce, in which the author described the feeding habits of the manta as follows: "When the giant ray dashes into a school of fish, the head fins are of great assistance in obtaining food, for like the arms of a boxer, they are in constant motion, whirling about and sweeping living prey into a yard-wide mouth with amazing facility as the giant hurls its body around in its natural element." Later, La Gorce identifies some authentic reports of devilfish running afoul of the anchor-chain: "True to instinct, it clasps the chain tight by wrapping its tentacula [*sic*] horns or feelers about it, applies its tremendous strength, lifts the heavy chain as if it were a feather, and starts to sea with the anchor, chain and ship, to the amazement and terror of the crew."

All of that is nonsense, of course, since the manta actually feeds by swimming slowly through schools of plankton and inhaling these microorganisms with the help of its guiding cephalic fins. But in the early decades of this century, there was little understanding of the biology of the manta and even less sensitivity to the plight of the hunted animal.[†] When La Gorce and his cronies harpooned a dolphin for sport off Bimini, the game was interrupted once the captain spotted a disturbance in the distance. It turned out to be a huge manta, which they harpooned with three irons. When the giant ray did not succumb, they shot it with a high-powered rifle. "It was a grand battle," wrote La Gorce, "full of thrills for each of us, although a little tough on the devilfish."

In the Sea of Cortez around 1976, scuba divers first discovered that the giant rays were so docile that, as they swam gently through clear waters, they could be ridden like living flying carpets. Many divers did so—and had themselves photographed doing it—but perhaps the best known of these manta riders was Peter Benchley, whose manta-riding picture (taken by Stan Waterman) serves as the author photo on the back cover of his novel *The Girl of the Sea of Cortez*. In this book, Benchley changed tactics to the point where the large sea creature—in this case a manta that had become entangled in a fisherman's net—is rescued by a girl named Paloma, but unlike the shark in *Jaws*, the ray is "the good guy." Like Androcles's lion, the manta saves the girl's life. Later, he even thanks her for cutting him free of the net by taking her to a previously undiscovered oyster bed where, we assume, giant pearls abound.

† By the time Marine Studios (later Marineland of Florida) opened in St. Augustine in June 1938, the curators had managed to capture two mantas for exhibition. They had so little information on the feeding habits of the giant rays that they crammed the mantas' mouths with mullet until they died.

SAWFISH

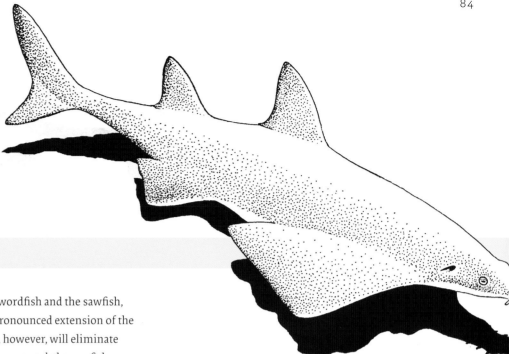

IT IS POSSIBLE TO CONFUSE THE swordfish and the sawfish, since both are very large fish with a pronounced extension of the upper jaw. A simple look at the name, however, will eliminate any confusion: The swordfish possesses a *sword*, the sawfish a *saw*. Easy as that. As we will see, the swordfish's use of its weapon is still speculative, as it is difficult to imagine the fish slicing and dicing its prey. Furthermore, nobody has ever seen a swordfish in action. If possible, the sawfish has an even stranger extension: a horizontally flattened blade studded with evenly spaced teeth on its outer margins. As with the mystery of the sword, it is not immediately evident how this creature might employ its weapon, but there is no question that it *is* a weapon. It is not, of course, used to saw its prey in half, and stories of the sawfish cutting large lumps of flesh from the bodies of fish are equally without foundation, although the otherwise dependable Norman and Fraser wrote in their *Giant Fishes, Whales and Dolphins* (1937), "On occasion it may even attack larger fishes, cutting large lumps of flesh from their bodies with the 'saw,' but stories of sawfish attacking whales are probably without foundation." (The authors also repeat a story of an Indian "Saw-fish [that] had once cut a bather entirely in two," but this must be treated as a baseless exaggeration, with no semblance of fact.)

Still, a twenty-foot-long fish equipped with what appears to be significant offensive armament is going to engender a lot of fish stories. For example, in *Sea and Land*, his 1887 compilation of animal folktales, J. W. Buel recounts the tale of a "saw-fish" caught by a Dr. Quackenbush of Mayport, Florida. Upon feeling a tug on his line, the fisherman, who was accompanied by his nine-year-old daughter, tried to reel in the unknown fish, when, "suddenly shot up a saw-bill four feet in length, and began striking, apparently blindly, from side to side until it reached the boat, when, with one terrific stroke, it tore away two feet of the stern down to the water's edge.... With admirable presence of mind, [Quackenbush] drives an oar into the infuriated fish's mouth with such force as to repel the vicious attack."

Alas, the sawfish is considerably less antagonistic than Mr. Buel would have us believe. Sawfish are actually slow-swimming bottom-feeders, usually found close to shore in shallow water, where they use the saw for digging up sand and mud to uncover buried shellfish (the rostrum of the sawfish has a similar electrical sensitivity to the head lobes of the hammerhead shark), although they have been known to slash at a school of mullet to injure or kill them. The sawfish (there are several species of the genus *Pristis*), in fact, is a shark-shaped ray, one of the cartilaginous fish that, for the most part, are characterized by a flattened rhomboid shape, with gills and mouth on the underside of the head. The pectoral fins are broad and emerge directly from the head, a sure indication of its affiliation with the rays. It has two large, evenly matched dorsal fins and a broad, sharklike tail fin with no caudal notch. (There are also several species of sawsharks, which can be differentiated from the sawfish by their smaller size; the presence of a pair of long, sensory barbels located midway along the snout; and gill slits that are on the sides of the head, as with most sharks.) Sawfish are live-bearers, but when the young are born, the saw is soft and rubbery, with the teeth embedded in it.

ABOVE *The sawfish (actually a kind of ray) with its gill slits and mouth on the underside of its head. It is believed that the saw is used to slash at its prey, which consists of small fish.*

Because they are not considered game fish, there are few records kept of their maximum length or weight, but they have been reliably reported at sixteen to eighteen feet in length, and at a weight of eight hundred pounds. They can be found in shallow waters along both coasts of Florida and Central America, throughout the Caribbean, and as far south as Brazil. The really big ones, it seems, are found off Panama.

In the early 1920s, British sportsman F. A. Mitchell-Hedges set out on a two-year fishing expedition, which he chronicled in *Battles with Giant Fish* (1923). Among the fish he claimed to have battled were a 40-pound snook, a 98-pound jack, a 1,300-pound hammerhead shark, a 1,460-pound "shovelnose shark," a great white shark, a 200-pound "porpoise" (from the photograph, a juvenile bottlenose dolphin, which he believed was a kind of fish), and finally, somewhere off Panama, a giant sawfish, harpooned by one of his "native boys." As the fish approached the shore, Mitchell-Hedges and Lady Richmond Brown splashed through the surf and hauled it in with a stout line. Then Mitchell-Hedges "smashed home two bullets where I thought its heart might be," killing it instantly. They measured the brute, and it was twenty-four feet six inches in length and seventeen feet six inches in girth, weighing 1.75 tons. But this was a bantamweight compared with the "leviathan of the deep" that Mitchell-Hedges captured on his last day fishing.

This monster towed Mitchell-Hedges and company all over the sea for more than six hours, but this time they managed to fasten the line around some rocks on shore. Once again, Mitchell-Hedges shot the fish, which, in its death throes, "reared up and then smashed straight down flat with a terrific spank on the water, while the brute gave two or three convulsive shudders." This brute was thirty-one feet long and weighed 5,700 pounds. If the book did not have photos of Mitchell-Hedges, Lady Brown, and a couple of really big sawfish, I would not believe a word of it. (It is easy to imagine measuring a thirty-one-foot-long fish on a remote beach in Panama, but how could the trigger-happy Mitchell-Hedges *weigh* his catch?)

As with so many of the big fish, the sawfish is currently in trouble. Although there was never a directed fishery for them, the toothed saws have always made desirable souvenirs, and whenever one was caught—accidentally or on purpose—the saw was made into a trophy. A nineteenth-century survey identified sawfish as among the most abundant species in the Indian River system of Florida; one mullet fisherman reported catching three hundred in a single season. So many sawfish were trapped in the nets of shrimp trawlers in the 1960s in the Gulf of Mexico that these accidental catches soon dropped to zero. "Even among biologists," wrote Janet Raloff in 2007, "these fish were 'never on the radar screen'… so their virtual disappearance in the 1970s went unnoticed." The same madness that has doomed so many sharks has also been responsible for the catastrophic decline in sawfish numbers around the world: The fins can be made into shark-fin soup. Because they are now rare, the fins of sawfish can command higher prices than those of sharks; a pair of the matched dorsal fins might be worth $3,000. In 2007, all international trade in sawfish was banned. It remains to be seen, however, if the treaty can protect the sawfish from those entrepreneurs who continue to catch them for their valuable fins and their toothy rostrum.

RIGHT *Sawfish were once common in the shallow waters of Florida and the Caribbean, but now they are endangered.*

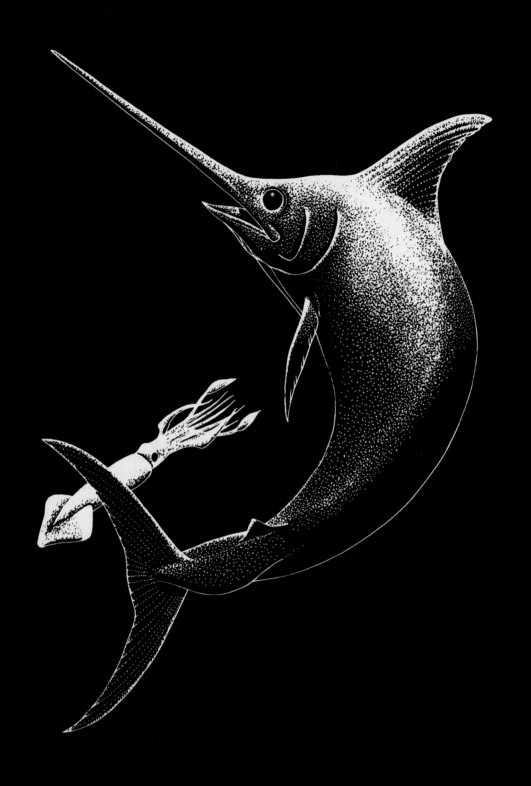

BIG-GAME FISH

Swordfish

Marlin

Sailfish

Bluefin Tuna

Yellowfin Tuna

SWORDFISH

THE BILLFISH INCLUDE THE SAILFISH and marlin, which comprise the family Istiophoridae, and the swordfish, the only member of the family Xiphiidae. They are characterized by a distinctive "bill" that gives each fish its unmistakable profile. The combination of size, beauty, and a ferocious reluctance to be reeled in defines billfish as the world's most important game fish. They are all large—some are among the largest and heaviest of all fish—but it is their matchless jumping and fighting ability that makes them especially worthy opponents for fishermen. Yes, a hooked tarpon or salmon will leap enthusiastically, but a thousand-pound marlin "tail-walking" or "greyhounding" along the surface represents the ultimate thrill for the deep-sea angler. The billfish are also known for their aggressiveness—swordfish are notorious for their attacks on boats, and divers in marlin-infested waters know enough to steer clear of these predators.

An adult swordfish is a graceful, tapered teardrop of a fish, with a formidable projectile point at one end and a huge crescent-shaped tail at the other. The tail, the fish's engine, is set perpendicular to a pair of fleshy keels on the tail stock, which are believed to impart speed and power to the tail. These lunate keels are also characteristic of tuna, sailfish, and mako sharks, other

contenders for the title of fastest fish in the sea. The swordfish's dorsal fin is a high sickle blade, situated far forward; its pectoral fins are long and gracefully curved. It has no ventral fins—no plumelike appendages like those of marlins and sailfish. The remaining complement of fins consists of a fleshy anal fin, as well as two small taglike fins atop and on the underside of the caudal peduncle. These last seem to be afterthoughts—but as there are no extraneous elements in fish design, they are probably hydrodynamically important in ways we do not understand.

Swordfish, found in temperate and tropical waters worldwide, are not the largest of all teleostean fishes—if we are going by length, the flimsy oarfish, at twenty-six feet, can be nearly twice as long—but if weight is the criterion, the broadbill is right up there with the big boys (actually big *girls*, because any billfish that weighs more than three hundred pounds is a female). The IGFA record book tells us that the heaviest bony fish ever caught—at least in compliance with IGFA rules—is a 1,560-pound black marlin that was reeled in off Cabo Blanco, Peru, in 1953. Other contenders are a bluefin tuna caught off Nova Scotia in 1979 that weighed 1,496 pounds and a 1,376-pound blue marlin that was caught off Hawaii in 1982. Compared to these three-quarter-ton monsters, the world-record swordfish was a relative lightweight at 1,182 pounds, but still, a fish that weighs more than half a ton is a very big fish indeed. The first one-thousand-pound fish—colloquially known as a "grander"—was a marlin caught by Zane Grey in Tahitian waters in 1930. The fish weighed 1,040 pounds, even after some 200 pounds by Grey's estimate was gnawed off by sharks before the fish was boated;

PREVIOUS SPREAD *One of the favorite prey items of the broadbill swordfish is the Humboldt squid,* Dosidicus gigas.

OPPOSITE *Sometimes seen sunning at the surface, the broadbill swordfish is also capable of dives to 4,000 feet.*

Big-game fisherman Michael Lerner poses proudly with two swordfish he caught on the same day off the coast of Chile in 1940.

with uncharacteristic reserve, he wrote, "best to have the record stand at the actual weight," without allowance for what he had lost.

Female swordfish grow faster and live longer than males. They reach their maximum size (one thousand pounds or more) at about fifteen years of age, but they are sexually mature at about the age of five. A female swordfish releases three to sixteen million eggs per spawning; after the eggs are fertilized, they will take two and a half days to hatch. Upon hatching, the larval swordfish is only a quarter inch in length and feeds on its fellow planktons. (Anything larger than the tiny swordfish might eat it, too.) Larval swordfish are spiky little devils; Myron Gordon called them "barb-wire fortresses." Swordfish larvae grow rapidly, faster than most other fish, and retain their larval characteristics until they are at least 7.5 inches long. As the baby swordfish grows, it goes through a series of morphological changes, and what begins as a full-length dorsal fin grows shorter until it becomes the tall, curved scimitar of the adult. The jaws enlarge, and then the lower jaw diminishes, resulting in a long upper jaw (the sword) and the "normal" lower jaw. Swordfish are born with teeth, proportional in size to their owner, but as the fish approach maturity, the teeth disappear, and the upper jaw begins to develop into a sword.

The broadbill swordfish gets its common name from this smooth, flattened bill, which is much longer and wider than that of any other billfish. We believe that the bill is used for defense and to slash and debilitate its prey, which consist of squid, mackerel, bluefish, and many other mid- and deepwater species. But even today, we are not sure how a swordfish actually deploys

its bill. It is horizontally flattened and sharp on the edges, so it has been assumed that the swordfish enters a school of fish and slashes wildly, cutting, stunning, or otherwise incapacitating the prey items, which it then eats at its leisure. Since few people have ever actually witnessed this activity, however, the technique must remain conjectural. In a 1968 study of "The Food and Feeding Habits of the Swordfish," W. B. Scott and S. N. Tibbo wrote, "The swordfish differs from the spearfishes (marlins and sailfishes) in that the sword is long and it is dorso-ventrally compressed (hence the name broadbill), whereas the spearfishes have a shorter spear and it is slightly compressed laterally. Thus, the swordfish appears to be more highly specialized for lateral slashing. Such a specialization would seem to be pointless unless directed to a vertically oriented prey, or unless the swordfish slashes while vertically oriented, as when ascending or descending." But Ralph Bandini, a renowned fisherman and one of the founding members of the Tuna Club of Catalina, saw a broadbill "cut a barracuda in half, *in the water*, as cleanly as it could be done with a butcher's cleaver on the block." Bandini does not mention the angle of attack, but it is clear that the broadbill's sharp-edged sword can be used with terrible effectiveness on smaller fish—or on other swordfish. In the introduction to a 1981 paper on the behavior of swordfish, Frank Carey and Bruce Robison include a fascinating note about an interspecies attack: "We have seen penetrating wounds in swordfish, and Edlin [pers. comm.] found a 15cm fragment of a swordfish bill that entered near the heart of a 70 kg [150 pound] swordfish and was driven back into the body cavity, which may indicate that they strike each other."

There are films in which one can see predators such as sharks, dolphins, sailfish, and marlins—sometimes even working together—feeding on "balled" baitfish. The predators herd a group of fish into a very tight ball, and the fish start to spin rapidly, like an underwater whirlwind—each fish trying to get to the center of the ball so as not to be the one that is eaten. The writhing ball makes it impossible for the predator to select an individual prey item, but having all the food bunched together gives a great advantage to the feeder. If the predator is armed with a rapier, charging the ball enables the billfish to kill many of the baitfish, and if it were to toss its head while its spear is in the "ball," even more baitfish would be bashed and slashed. No one has ever observed swordfish in the act of capturing their prey, but if they were to be seen attacking baitballs, some of the mysteries of swordfish feeding would be solved. Oblivious to our difficulties in understanding (or observing) the process, swordfish obviously manage to feed themselves quite efficiently.

How they eat is a problem for conjecture, but *what* they eat can be determined by the relatively simple expedient of catching the swordfish and examining the contents of its stomach. Analyzing the stomach contents of fifty-eight females and twenty-four males taken in the Azorean longline fishery, Patricia Ribeiro Simões and José Pedro Andrade of the University of Algarve, Portugal, found that male and female swordfish have different diets. The cutlassfish (*Lepidopus caudatus*), an aggressive species, reaching up to seven feet in length, was predominantly found in the stomachs of females; the boarfish (*Capros aper*), reaching only about six inches in length and living in schools near the surface, was the favorite fish of male swordfish in Azorean waters. In general, it was the smaller fish, such as lanternfish (Myctophidae), that mainly showed up in the stomachs of males.

Although they occasionally bask at the surface in full sun, swordfish prefer to dwell in semidarkness. They dive deep at the first glow of morning and rise at dusk, just as the sun begins to set. Their huge eyes, as big as grapefruit, are so sensitive that the fish respond to moonlight. When the swordfish descends to hunt, its body cools slowly. During these daily migrations, the swordfish encounters extreme changes in water temperature. Cold temperatures impair the nervous system, and one would expect these broad swings to render the swordfish stuporous, but in a 1992 article in *Oceanus*, Frank Carey, who believed that a six-hundred-pound swordfish could stay below the thermocline for days, describes the "temperature tricks" that the swordfish employs. Carey's studies showed that the swordfish's eye muscles and tiny brain ("about as big as the last joint of my index finger") are swaddled in a mass of brown tissue ("about the size of a hen's egg") the color and consistency of liver. This brown blanket is suffused with warm blood from its own large rete mirabile and is built from modified muscle cells, which produce heat. The organ is fifty times larger than the swordfish brain and pumps out enough heat to raise the fish's cranial temperature well above the surrounding water. And since swordfish spend a lot of time in deep, cold water, all of this effort is not wasted. Unlike the flesh of the tuna, which is predominantly red muscle with a heavy concentration of mitochondria and myoglobin that provides energy for endurance activities, the flesh of swordfish is mostly white muscle, which is designed for sudden bursts of activity. Swordfish generally move with prevailing currents, where they use their acute vision to locate their prey and their superior acceleration to chase it down.

Undoubtedly due to its size and armament, the swordfish has always been regarded as a dangerous creature, and probably always will be. Here, for example, is the description of *"Xyphias gladius communis"* from William Dewhurst's 1835 *Natural History of the Order Cetacea and the Oceanic Inhabitants of the Arctic Regions*: "The common sword-fish is a native of the Mediterranean and Sicilian Seas; it grows to a very large size, sometimes measuring twenty feet in length; it is active and predacious, feeding on all kinds of fishes, and it is likely a formidable enemy to the whale, which it destroys by piercing it with its sword-shaped snout." Never mind about mercury—which may be present in greater amounts in swordfish than any other food fish—this is a fish that can kill you.

In his *Memoirs of the Royal Asiatic Society of Bengal* (1940), E. W. Gudger wrote a paper titled, "The Alleged Pugnacity of the Swordfish and the Spearfishes as Shown by Their Attacks on Vessels." He wrote that, in some cases, swordfish charge the boats from which they have been harpooned or hooked, but in other cases, such as attacks on whales, bales of rubber, or submarines, the attack comes out of the blue, as it were, with no identifiable motivating factors. Even sharks, long considered mindless man-eaters, do not attack people randomly or accidentally. Something moves them to bite: It may be fear, hunger, territoriality, electrical stimulation, or confusion about what is edible or what is not, but most people do not consider sharks malicious or evil, but simply—as if this actually needed saying—animals that are profoundly different from us.

Most animal behavior studies do not involve attacks on people; but when tigers eat people, sharks kill surfers, or swordfish attack divers, we are forced to reconsider our attitude toward very big, very heavily armed animals. On April 15, 2003, Mark Ferrari was swimming in water 250 feet deep in the AuAu Channel between the Hawaiian islands of Maui and

Mark Ferrari took this photograph just before the swordfish turned and stabbed him.

Lanai. A whale researcher and filmmaker, Ferrari had been working for years in these waters with his wife, and fellow researcher, Debbie Glockner-Ferrari. Their primary interest was the behavior of humpback whales, but on this day, Mark was following a school of false killer whales (*Pseudorca crassidens*), rarely photographed toothed whales that are closely related to pilot whales and killer whales. In the clear blue water, off to his right about thirty feet away, he spotted a shadow, not as large as the false killers, but of a completely different configuration. From its protruding snout and vertical tail fin, he recognized it as a billfish, about fifteen feet long. Because female billfish are larger than males, and because this was a *very* large specimen, Mark assumed it was a female. Was it a swordfish? A marlin? He shot a couple of frames of the fish, which seemed to be hovering in the water about twenty feet away. When he lost sight of the false killers and the fish, he thought the encounter was over and climbed back into the boat.

At the surface, the black false killers were leaping excitedly, and Mark decided to reenter the water to see what was going on. Big mistake. The *Pseudorcas* had formed a sort of net beneath the billfish, and every time she tried to escape by diving, one of them rushed in and bit a chunk from her flank. Mark was now ten feet from the wounded fish, and for a reason that will never be known, she charged directly at him. Was it mindless panic? A defensive maneuver aimed at whatever she could hit? He was struck high on his right chest, just at the base of the neck; his clavicle was broken and his scapula shattered. The sword, some of which had broken off in Mark's body, had missed his carotid artery by less than half an inch—a little lower and it would have punctured his lung. The sword did not pass through him, and with a toss of her head, the fish disengaged and swam off. Bleeding badly, Mark surfaced and called for Debbie, who was in the boat not far away. Once ashore, they loaded him into an ambulance, held wet towels over the gaping wound, and drove him across the island to Maui Memorial Hospital in Wailuku. In addition to the broken bones, there was extensive nerve and muscle damage. He had lost so much blood that the surgeons thought he might not make it.

Ferrari is one of a comparatively small number of humans to have seen the billfish in its habitat. Aquarists have maintained almost everything else, from whale sharks, white sharks, sawfish, and even bluefin tuna, in tanks for public observation. The one-million-gallon "Outer Bay" tank at the Monterey Bay Aquarium in California is home to dozens of large bluefin and yellowfin tuna, and from September 14, 2004, to March 31, 2005, a juvenile great white shark was housed there before being released back into the ocean. There have been only two large whales ever held in captivity; they were gray whales, both of which were captured as juveniles, both of which were kept at Sea World in San Diego, and released when they got too big for any tank and too expensive to feed. To date, there have been no successful attempts to capture a coelacanth; most large squid are too excitable to be kept in captivity (they tend to jump out of tanks) and the idea of exhibiting a billfish is almost oxymoronic. You cannot capture one except by fishing for it, a process that inevitably injures the fish, and even if you could somehow get one into a tank, its temperament and armament seem designed for tank- or self-destruction.

Shortly after *The Book of Sharks* appeared in 1975, I was asked by ABC-TV's *American Sportsman* if I would like to go shark fishing with Peter Benchley aboard Frank Mundus's *Cricket II*. I had done this once before, but Mundus was such a wonderful character, and Peter Benchley such a great friend, that I jumped at the opportunity. With a full TV crew (two cameramen, a soundman, and a producer) we boarded the *Cricket II*, and set out. It was a brilliant April morning—the kind of day the fishermen call a "bluebird day"—and when the Montauk lighthouse had faded from sight, we set the first rods. Captain Mundus was now famous, too, because he believed that the character "Quint" in *Jaws* was based on him, and he took every opportunity to behave like a lunatic— which he surely was not—in front of the cameras. He sported a pirate's hoop earring (more unusual in 1975 than now), and wore one red sock and one green one to differentiate port and starboard. In addition, he kept a loaded rifle handy, to dispatch the dangerous sharks if they gave us any trouble.

Benchley, now a full-fledged literary lion because of the astonishing success of his novel, was to have the first shot, so he strapped himself into the fighting chair, and let the line play out. It was only a matter of minutes before he felt a strike, and he began the back-breaking process of reeling in a very heavy and

Outnumbering their potential prey, two makos home in on a lone swordfish.

close to the surface, he saw that it was iridescent in a way that no shark was supposed to be. Mundus was still lecturing Benchley on the dangerous shark he was bringing up, but when the fish broke the surface Pat recognized it, and with the cameras running and the microphones recording, he shouted, "That son of a bitch is a swordfish!"

We gaffed the swordfish and brought it aboard, and the whole "shark fishing" episode had to be repeated. Both Benchley and I later caught blue sharks on camera, but they were not nearly as exciting as that first-strike swordfish. The fish weighed upward of 250 pounds, so when we docked, it was butchered and we took home a trunkful of swordfish steaks, along with the film of our expedition. Even in 1976, large swordfish were becoming scarce because of overfishing. The average weight of swordfish caught since the 1980s has dropped from 115 pounds to 60. Today, many restaurants refuse to put swordfish on their menus in an attempt to discourage fishermen from bringing in the smaller fish. (At New York City's Fulton Fish Market, swordfish that are between 50 and 100 pounds are called "dogs"; from 25 to 50, "pups"; and under 25 pounds, "rats.") In "Song for the Swordfish," a 1998 article in *Audubon* magazine, Carl Safina wrote, "These days, most fishers know swordfish chiefly by their absence, by old-timers' stories and black-and-white photos on the walls of long-established harborside bars. The swordfish, also known as the broadbill, may be the fastest-declining creature in the Atlantic Ocean.... U.S. longliners claim that Atlantic swordfish can't recover unless all the countries catching them agree to coordinated measures." In 1975, though, we were unaware of these controversies, and were delighted with our serendipitous catch. It was a time of innocence, when few people recognized the threats to the oceans' wildlife.

very reluctant fish. Because this was all being filmed, Mundus was supposed to be talking about the shark on the line, and, never at a loss for words, he guided Benchley through the process. At this stage, of course, we had no idea what was on the end of the line, but Mundus talked as if it were a shark, and maybe even the kind that Benchley had recently made so famous: "OK, now take it slow ... reel it in as you lean forward, then put your back into it ... sharks have skin like sandpaper, so if he gets tangled in the line, he'll snap it like a thread ... white sharks are dangerous even when they're hooked." While the cameramen filmed the fishermen on the afterdeck, Pat Smith, the producer/director, had climbed up onto the flying bridge so he could see the whole scene that was playing out below. That vantage point put him in a position to see the fish before anyone else did, and when it was

MARLIN

The black marlin, shown here chasing yellowfin tuna, can reach a weight of 1,500 pounds and is probably the world's most sought-after big-game fish.

JUST AS THE SWORDFISH GETS ITS name from the resemblance of its upper jaw to a sword, the marlin gets its common name from the marlinspike, a pointed iron tool from the days of sail that was used to separate strands of rope—sometimes known as "marlines"—in splicing. (There are even some references to "marlinspike swordfish.") There may be three species of marlin—or four, or five, or sixteen. The confusion was exacerbated by big-game-fishing writers such as Zane Grey and Ernest Hemingway, who used different common names for different species: Grey liked to call marlins "marlin swordfish," for example, and it is likely that neither of them knew (or cared) how many large marlin species there were; they paid only passing attention to scientific nomenclature.

In Grey's *Tales of Tahitian Waters*, we find this mystifying sequence: "When we arrived at our dock we pulled the swordfish ashore and strung him up. He was a superb specimen of the ordinary striped marlin spearfish." In 1930, Grey decided to name his 1,040-pounder a "Giant Tahitian Striped Marlin," but in a 1935 note, J. T. Nichols and Francesca LaMonte confounded the nomenclature even further, as they decided that "the Tahitian black marlin, or silver marlin swordfish," caught by Eastham Guild in 1931 (the photograph had been sent to them by Zane Grey), was "a recognizable undescribed form."

In *Billfishes of the World* (1985), Izumi Nakamura, a billfish expert from Japan, identifies the following marlin species: the black marlin (*Makaira indica*), the Indo-Pacific blue marlin (*M. mazara*), the Atlantic blue marlin (*M. nigricans*), the Atlantic white marlin (*Tetrapterus albidus*), and the striped marlin

TOP *Alfred Glassell poses with his world-record 1,560-pound black marlin, caught off Cabo Blanco, Peru, in 1953.*

BOTTOM *Zane Grey's Tahitian marlin would have been a world record if sharks hadn't removed some two hundred pounds of meat as Grey was towing it in.*

(*T. audax*). The first two, at lengths in excess of fourteen feet and with recorded weights above 1,300 pounds, are the largest of the group. The various species are characterized by different markings and ranges, but stripes and lateral-line configurations notwithstanding, all marlins are very much alike. The dorsal fin is high just behind the shoulders—and these fish certainly can be said to have shoulders—and has a long, low base, trailing all the way back to the small second dorsal. The main dorsal can be laid back, unlike the high dorsal of the swordfish, which is permanently erect. Where the swordfish has a single, wide keel on each side of the base of its crescent-shaped tail, the marlins have two smaller keels on each side. The marlins' sword is stout at the base and round in cross section, tapering to a rapierlike point. The sword of the blue marlin is proportionally longer and narrower than that of the black; the black marlin's sword is thicker and heavier, often with a slight downturn. Marlins have small, file-like teeth and a lateral line that cannot be seen unless the elongated, densely packed scales or skin are removed. The adult swordfish has no scales, no teeth, and no lateral line, even under the skin, but all marlins have teeth and a lateral line, although the term "line" is rather loosely applied to this wiggly article. As with the swordfish, in all species of marlins, females grow considerably larger than males.

Marlins are found throughout the world's offshore temperate oceans, usually in (or over) deep water. When they hatch, newborn marlins bear little resemblance to the adults. They are bug-eyed little creatures, with a sail-like dorsal fin and large, wide pectorals. As they mature, the dorsal changes into the familiar form, the pectorals become sickle-shaped, and the upper jaw begins to assume the spearlike shape that characterizes the genus. Larvae have been measured at a half inch in length, and assuming that nothing interrupts the growth curve—a dangerous assumption where tiny fish are concerned—they will keep growing, perhaps for as long as ten years, until they reach their massive adulthood.

It is possible to visualize a swordfish charging into a tightly packed school of fish, slashing as it goes with its sharp sword, but the rounded bill of the marlins presents more of a problem. Does the marlin wield its sword like a club, clobbering fish senseless before gobbling them up? All the istiophorids are powerful swimmers and they have teeth; they feed by chasing down their prey. They are known to dine on fast-swimming, relatively large fish such as dolphins and tuna, so they must be able to catch and capture them in the open sea. Pelagic squid, also fast-swimming creatures, capable of leaping out of the ocean to escape their pursuers, have been found in the stomachs of captured marlins. Nakamura reports that a fisheries biologist working on the Sea of Cortez, off Baja California, saw a large blue marlin approach a school of Humboldt squid (*Dosidicus gigas*) "that was gathering under the night light of a squid-fishing boat; it approached the school at almost full speed with its fins completely held back in the grooves, then suddenly hit the squids with its bill, subsequently nudging the stunned prey and eating it head first." A picture of the great marlin as a superpredator is beginning to emerge: This is a fish that will eat anything it can catch, and it can catch just about anything that swims.

A sun-dappled marlin cruises near the surface.

SAILFISH

"SWORDFISH," which was incorporated into Zane Grey's *Tales of Fishes* (1919), George Brown Goode writes about the names of the sailfish:

> The "sailfish," Histiophorus americanus, *is called by sailors in the South the "boohoo" or "woohoo." This is evidently a corrupted form of "guebum," a name, apparently of Indian origin, given to the same fish in Brazil. It is possible that* Tetrapturus *is also called "boohoo," since the two genera are not sufficiently unlike to impress sailors with their differences. Blecker states that in Sumatra the Malays call the related species,* H. gladius, *by the name "Joohoo" (Juhu), a curious coincidence. The names may have been carried from the Malay Archipelago to South America, or vice versa, by mariners.*

Whatever its name in South America or Sumatra, the boohoo, woohoo, or joohoo is now officially known as *Istiophorus albicans* in the Atlantic and *Istiophorus platypterus* in the Pacific and Indian Oceans. (*Istiophorus* means "sail-bearer," from the Greek *histion* for "sail.") Many believe there is only a single, worldwide species (*Istiophorus platypterus*), but if there are indeed two species, they are very similar. (In *Billfishes of the World*, the same drawing is used to illustrate both species.) The maximum size of a sailfish is ten feet, and the world-record (Pacific) sailfish, caught off Ecuador in 1947, weighed 221 pounds. The Atlantic record is 141 pounds. In *Fishing the Pacific* (1953), Kip Farrington describes the two kinds of sailfish: "The bill of the Pacific sailfish is much longer and more tapered than that of the Atlantic variety. The sail is much larger in proportion to his size and the ventral fin much longer. The coloring is exquisite, and no other fish that I have seen, except the Allison tuna, the dolphin, and striped marlin, is more beautiful than the Pacific sailfish as it dies. The light blue sheen is indescribable. This is a gallant little fish and I have great admiration for him."

Sailfish are marlin-shaped but slimmer, with a sharp spear that is round in cross section; a blue-backed, silver-bellied color scheme with a pattern of vertical stripes; double keels on the tail stock; and a large, lunate tail fin. But where the marlins have a fairly modest dorsal fin, the sailfish have the great towering sail that gives them their name, an appendage unlike that of any other fish in the sea. The actual function of the sail is unknown, but we do know that it can be laid flat on the fish's back when the

PREVIOUS PAGE *The author's father with a good-sized sailfish caught off Cuba in 1950.*

fish rockets through the water, and there are records of a sailfish being clocked at sixty-eight miles per hour. Mark Ferrari might be inclined to award the title "world's fastest fish" to the broadbill swordfish that stabbed him, but certain tuna and the wahoo have also been nominated. It is difficult to calculate the speed of a fish in the water, but even if this could be done, how would we know that the fish is swimming at its maximum speed? We would not, of course, but on a 1964 research cruise off the Pacific coast of Costa Rica, Vladimir Walters and Harry Fierstine designed a device that measures the speed of a line as it is taken out by recently hooked yellowfin tuna and wahoo, and found that in the first ten to twenty seconds, they were each clocked at around forty-six to forty-seven miles per hour.

Whether the dorsal fin contributes to these speeds or not, authorities believe that the sailfish gets its name from this fin's resemblance to a sail (albeit a sort of spiky one, with all those fin rays); J. B. Tinsley, however, in *The Sailfish, Swashbuckler of the Open Seas* (1964), goes further by citing Sir Thomas Raffles, the British East Indian administrator of the Napoleonic era who claimed to have seen the sailfish *sailing*, its dorsal fin raised to catch the wind. And later, no less a pair of authorities than Norman and Fraser, in their *Giant Fishes, Whales, and Dolphins* (1936), quote Raffles's description, although they do not verify it: "The only amusing discovery which we have recently made is that of the sailing fish, called by the natives *ikan layer*, about ten or twelve feet long, which hoists a mainsail, and often sails in the manner of a native boat, and with considerable swiftness." It seems more likely that a sailfish will occasionally lie at the surface with its sail fanned out, sunning itself like a swordfish, and while the sail acts as a heat absorber, it might—by accident, surely—catch the wind.

Underwater films have been made of the sailfish with its sail raised to its full height, corralling a school of baitfish, then charging the school and striking with its sword. The raised sail may also have something to do with mating; Nakamura wrote, "Around Florida, this species often moves inshore where the females, swimming sluggishly with their dorsal fins extended and accompanied each by one or more males, may spawn near the surface in the warm season."

The spear of the sailfish is smaller and more slender than that of the marlins, and in no way resembles the flattened weapon of the swordfish, so it is occasionally possible to identify a fish that has pierced a boat when its bill breaks off. Gudger's survey, published in 1940, contains no specific records of sailfish attacks on boats, but Tinsley's book, devoted as it is to everything sailfish, includes several. The first known attack, he tells us, took place in 1725, when the HMS *Leopard* put in to Portsmouth for repairs and the narrow bayonet of a sailfish was found in the ship's bottom, having penetrated the vessel's one-inch-thick sheathing, three inches of planking, and another four inches of timber, for a total of eight inches. He quotes the early American big-game fisherman, Charles Frederick Holder, who wrote about sailfish in 1914, as follows: "These magnificent fish are harpooned by the natives of Madagascar and often wreck the boats and kill the men. An American consul saw one leap through the sail of a native proa—and described the fight to me." Tinsley cites several other sailfish attacks on native fishermen and their boats, but it is clear that the sailfish, blessed only with speed and beauty, is no match for the rhinolike charges of thousand-pound marlins or swordfish when it comes to attacking boats.

Today, *Istiophorus* is considered one of the world's premier game fish, but because it does not achieve the monster size of some of its relatives, it is popular with those who do not fancy themselves the type to fight a ton and a half of fish for half a day or more. The IGFA fly rod record for Atlantic sailfish is 94 pounds; for Pacific, it's 111 pounds. In Charles Mather's book *Billfish: Marlin, Broadbill, Sailfish* (1976), alongside a photograph of a young boy with two sailfish, it says: "Small Atlantic sailfish are great sport for small children." The IGFA record book account of the sailfish includes, "Its fighting ability and spectacular aerial acrobatics endear the sailfish to the saltwater angler, but it tires quickly and is considered a light-tackle species." But because of their brilliant coloration, spectacular acrobatics, and availability, sailfish are probably the most popular of all big-game fish.

OPPOSITE *Although it never comes close to the massive size of the blue and black marlins, the sailfish is still one of the world's most popular game fishes.*

BLUEFIN TUNA

THE TUNA IS REVERED FOR ITS BEAUTY and power, while at the same time, its nutritious and tasty flesh has made it the object of commercial fisheries for more than four thousand years. We know that the Phoenicians fished for tuna in the Mediterranean; Aristotle and Pliny wrote about ancient tuna fisheries, and well into the twenty-first century, Sicilians trapped them in "net-cities" off the island of Favignana. For its role in human history, the tuna puts the lowly codfish in the shade. Around the world, various tuna species are among the world's favorite food fish. Skipjack, albacore, and yellowfin tuna are killed by the billions every year so that people can eat tuna-fish salads and sandwiches. Around the world, fierce political battles are taking place for the "rights" to catch tuna, and because of these battles, the tuna, surely the paradigmatic innocent bystanders, are being pushed to the brink of extinction. In the early twentieth century, bluefin tuna were known as "horse mackerel," fit only to feed to dogs, but the astonishing development of the Japanese sashimi market turned the tuna from a trash fish into the most valuable fish in the world.

There are many kinds of fish commonly known as tuna—albacore, bigeye, dogtooth, yellowfin, skipjack, longtail, blackfin and the bluefin, which comes in three varieties: northern (*Thunnus thynnus*), Pacific northern (*Thunnus orientalis*), and southern (*Thunnus maccoyii*). All tuna are scombrids, but not all scombrids are tuna. The family Scombridae includes several species of smaller, bullet-shaped fish that are grouped with the tuna, and also the mackerel, which are essentially smallish tuna without the heft and without many of the advanced features that characterize the genus *Thunnus*. The Spanish mackerel, kingfish, seerfish, and the wahoo, a large, elongated game fish, famed for its speed and unwillingness to be landed, are also classified as scombrids. All scombrids are more or less pointed at both ends, with a crescent-shaped tail and a series of finlets on the dorsal and ventral surfaces of the hind end, aft of the second dorsal fin

and just before the insertion of the tail fin. The function of these finlets is unknown, but because all scombrids are fast swimmers, they are believed to be connected with a capacity for speed. Below the big-tuna designations, there are several species of bonitos, "little tuna," "bullet tuna," "frigate tuna," the kawakawa, and the cero. Most of the tuna are considered big-game fish, worthy of being chased by fishermen in big expensive boats, but all of the species that can exceed twenty pounds in weight are also popular food fish, and are the objects of some of the world's most extensive fisheries.

Unlike many other fish species that can gulp water into their mouths and over their gills, tuna are "ram ventilators," which means they have to keep moving or they will die. They have a suite of anatomical modifications that enable them to heat their muscles and their brains as much as thirty degrees above the surrounding water. With the swordfish, great white, mako, and porbeagle sharks, they are the only "warm-blooded" fish, which gives them a huge advantage over their prey. Bluefin tuna also have the largest gill surfaces of any fish. Not proportionally, absolutely: Because they are among the largest of all bony fish (the world record weighed 1,496 pounds and individuals can reach fourteen feet in length and thirty years in age), much of their description is couched in superlatives. They are among the fastest of all fish, having been clocked at fifty-five miles an hour. They can function at the surface and at three-quarters of a mile down. They are the longest known migrators of any fish species; Atlantic bluefins travel from New England to the Mediterranean, then turn around and swim back (remember, they can never stop swimming). In the North Pacific bluefins can make a round-trip from California to Japan and turn around and do it all over again.

For many bluefins today, in both oceans, the round-trip is over, as they are picked off along the way by longliners, purse seiners, tuna ranchers, sportfishermen, or harpooners. The Mediterranean Sea is the major breeding ground for bluefin tuna of the eastern North Atlantic. Where the bluefins came from was of little interest to Mediterranean fishers, who trapped schools of these great fish as they entered or left their sea for millennia. Every spring for centuries on the butterfly-shaped island of Favignana, off the northwest coast of Sicily, the local fishermen constructed elaborate offshore traps, using miles of cable, iron anchors, and nets fashioned into chambers, one

OPPOSITE *The northern bluefin tuna* (Thunnus thynnus) *is the largest and most powerful of the tuna clan, and can weigh three-quarters of a ton.*

leading into another. The nets slowly filled with migrating tuna; when enough had been trapped, the *rais*, the boss of the *tonnaroti*, announced that the *mattanza*—the massacre—was to begin. In the last chamber, known as the "chamber of death," men slammed ten-foot-long gaffs into the bodies of the tuna. The *mattanza* is mercifully over, not only because people objected to this barbarous practice but because the Mediterranean is running out of tuna. In September 2006, the World Wildlife Fund, fearful of the extinction of the species, called for a halt of all bluefin tuna fishing in the Mediterranean. "If nothing is done," said Paolo Guglielmi, of the World Wildlife Fund's Mediterranean Programme Office, "wild bluefin tuna will completely disappear from the Mediterranean, perhaps with no possibility of rebuilding stocks."

While there are strict international quotas on the number of bluefin tuna that can be caught in nets or by harpoons, there are no regulations whatsoever applied to the practice of "postharvesting" or "tuna ranching," which means catching half-grown wild tuna and fattening them in pens before they are slaughtered. There are postharvesting "farms" in the waters of practically every country on or in the Mediterranean, as well as on the coasts of Australia and Mexico, accounting for more tuna than are caught by direct fishing. More than 90 percent of the postharvested tuna goes to Japan, and the appetite of the Japanese for tuna-belly meat is insatiable. Killing off large numbers of animals before they reach breeding age is one of the best ways to reduce a population drastically, and the bluefin tuna is everywhere endangered.

On March 4, 2008, the South Australian tuna-ranching company Clean Seas announced that male and female bluefins in the breeding tank at Arno Bay had spawned. In an article in *The Australian* (2008), Chairman Hagen Stehr said, "We have proven what can be done, even with southern bluefin tuna, which is the holy grail of aquaculture…. In the future this will be a staggering industry of immense proportions. It depends on us, the state government and the federal government, how big we want this to be. In years to come, this will give us a sustainable bluefin industry, that no one in the world will be able to attack." Stehr's company has already shown that they can raise big fish such as yellowtail kingfish and mulloway from eggs, so raising bluefins should not be an insurmountable problem. Because there are no

quotas on fish raised artificially, Clean Seas can essentially set the market for tuna exported to Japan, China, Europe, and the United States. If they can raise the tuna to market size, there is essentially no limit on the amount they can sell. It will be years before the Clean Seas bluefins grow to marketable size, so we must wait to learn if the Australian captive-breeding program will arrive in time to rescue the Mediterranean bluefins from rapacious overfishing.

The big-game fisherman sees the bluefin tuna as a sleek and powerful opponent; to the harpooner it is an iridescent shadow below the surface, flicking its scythe-like tail to propel it out of range; the purse seiner sees a churning maelstrom of silver and blue bodies to be hauled on deck; the longliner sees a dead fish,

ABOVE *The bluefin tuna is a graceful, sleek projectile of a fish, capable of reaching speeds of 50 miles per hour.*

BELOW *"Them days are gone forever." Michael Lerner (center) with twenty-one bluefin tuna caught off Wedgeport, Nova Scotia, in 1935.*

OPPOSITE RIGHT *The current world-record bluefin was caught by Ken Fraser off Auld's Cove, Nova Scotia, in 1979, and weighed 1,496 pounds.*

hauled on deck along with other glistening marine creatures; the tuna rancher sees the bluefin as an anonymous creature to be force-fed until it is time to drive a spike into its brain; the auctioneer at Tsukiji fish market in Tokyo sees row upon row of tailless, ice-rimmed, tuna-shaped blocks; Japanese consumers see it as *toro*, a slice of rich red meat, to be eaten with wasabi and soy sauce; to the biologist the tuna is a marvel of hydrodynamic engineering, its body packed with modifications that enable it to

outeat, outgrow, outswim, outdive, and outmigrate any other fish in the sea; and to those who would rescue *Thunnus thynnus* from the oblivion of extinction, it has to be seen as a domesticated animal, like a sheep or a cow. For some, such a shift is almost impossible; the bluefin tuna, the quintessential ocean ranger, the wildest, fastest, most powerful fish in the sea, cannot be—and probably *should* not be—tamed. But if it is not, we will only be able to say that we loved the tuna not wisely, but too well.

YELLOWFIN TUNA

WITH ITS EXTREMELY LONG, CANARY yellow second dorsal and anal fins, the yellowfin (*Thunnus albacares*) is easily differentiated from other tuna. The pectoral fins, which also become yellow in adult fish, are very long, reaching to the base of the second dorsal. (Only the albacore has proportionally longer pectorals.) The little finlets between the fins and the tail are also bright yellow. The most brilliantly colored of the tuna, the yellowfin is metallic blue or greenish black above and pearl white below; in younger fish, the lower flanks are crossed with broken vertical lines. Adult fish have a band of bright gold or iridescent blue (sometimes both) running along the flank. Spawning yellowfins have been observed to "flash" their colors, perhaps as a stimulant to the opposite sex. Conversely, dying tuna begin to lose their bright coloration and soon fade to shades of dull gray.

Yellowfins are found in every ocean (except the Mediterranean) in a wide swath between 45°N and 40°S. At least some of the stocks are migratory. Because of their size and strength (a mature specimen can grow to seven feet in length and four hundred pounds), yellowfins are still highly regarded as game fish—few other species can reach their size and put up such a fight—and therefore they are among the primary objects of sport fisheries around the world. Like most tuna, the yellowfin is an extremely fast swimmer, clocked at around forty-six to forty-seven miles per hour from a standing start when hooked. Zane Grey knew that the yellowfin was fast (Zane Grey knew everything) and in 1925 he wrote of "tuna of three or four hundred pounds, shooting like a bullet through the water …." In *Fishing in Bermuda* (2003), James Faiella wrote, "The yellowfin is considered the most prized of all tuna varieties both around Bermuda and elsewhere for their size, gameness, and the high quality of their flesh." Peter Goadby, one of Australia's most articulate and influential fishermen, sings the praises of the yellowfin as a game fish:

> *The yellowfin is surely one of the fastest and most tenacious of all fish. The grab of a live bait or lure is followed by a preliminary run then, as if realizing that it is in trouble, the fish really claps on the pace, often sounding as it runs. Then the great circling fight begins with every foot of the line having to be won and held on the reel as the line shortens and the circles narrow and tighten. The time of the tail beats indicates the size of the fish …. Kip Farrington, one of the most experienced tuna fishermen, rated a 200 lb. yellowfin in deep water as the equivalent of other species, including bluefin, twice the weight.*

Goadby was talking about Australia, but charter boats and individual fishermen set out after yellowfins from San Diego, South Africa, the "Tuna Coast" of Panama, Hawaii, Costa Rica, Mexico, Honduras, Massachusetts, Cape Hatteras (North Carolina), Bermuda, various countries in or on the Caribbean, and throughout the South Pacific, from Thailand and French Polynesia to all Australian coasts.

Like many fish species, yellowfins are compulsive schoolers, but they often swim in mixed schools with skipjacks, bigeyes, and other tuna. Wherever yellowfins congregate, they are targeted by commercial fishers. Schooling yellowfins have a trait that would ultimately prove to be their undoing: They tend to aggregate near or under floating objects that can be as insignificant as a floating log, as large as a ship, or as active as a group of dolphins. In particular, and for reasons that are still unknown, yellowfins aggregate under schools of spotter and spinner dolphins in the eastern tropical Pacific, west of Central America and Mexico. In the 1960s, tuna fishermen out of San Diego using purse seines learned that they could locate schools of yellowfin tuna by scanning the horizons for disturbances on the surface made by herds of leaping dolphins. In the fishing technique called "setting on dolphins," a school of dolphins is rounded up like cattle by a small speedboat reeling out a wall of net that encircles the fish. Then, the net is closed ("pursed") by a cable and rings, and the net with the tuna and dolphins in it is winched aboard a large fishing boat standing by. One set might net anywhere from ten to one hundred tons of tuna, and this proved to be a much more productive method of fishing than the old hook-and-line fishing. Production increased dramatically, but so did the dolphin mortality. According to a 1986 study by N. C. H. Lo and Tim Smith, "the annual kill from 1959 to 1972 varied from 55,000 in 1959 to 534,000 in 1961. There were three distinct maxima of 534,000, 460,000 and 467,000, corresponding to peaks in the number of sets made on dolphins in 1961, 1965, and 1970. The total kill from 1959 to 1972 was estimated to be about 4.8 million."

A great environmental outcry resulted in the passage of the Marine Mammal Protection Act in 1972, which made it a violation in the United States to harm any cetacean, but the tuna fishermen lobbied for an exemption, and they continued to kill dolphins in staggering numbers—more than three hundred thousand died in 1972. The fishermen continued to set their nets "on dolphins" until they were sued in federal court by a consortium of conservation groups and forced to suspend their entire fishing operations. They were allowed to commence again only if they could abide by strict quotas imposed by the government, which were to be decreased annually to allow the fishermen to adjust to the new regulations. The first new quota, set in 1976, allowed the fishermen to kill seventy-eight thousand dolphins. The number was steadily reduced until it stood at twenty thousand by 1981. In 1990, the StarKist Seafood Company (a subsidiary of the conglomerate H. J. Heinz), announced that it would no longer purchase tuna that had been caught with

dolphins, and began to label cans of StarKist tuna "dolphin-safe." BumbleBee and Chicken of the Sea quickly followed suit, and because these three companies accounted for more than 80 percent of the tuna sold in the United States, the dolphins were spared—for the moment, anyway.

After skipjack, yellowfin is the second-heaviest fished of the tuna. Like skipjack, it is canned and marketed as "light" tuna, but it is also an important component of sushi and sashimi. (The only tuna that can be labeled "white" is albacore.) When cooked, yellowfin meat is firm and mild tasting, and it tends to have a very light yellowish brown color. In larger fish (twenty to thirty pounds) the meat tends to become slightly darker and drier. A report issued by the Japanese Fishing Authority in 2005 analyzed recent trends in tuna fishing in the Western and Central Pacific. In 2004, 1,447 longliners, 176 pole-and-line boats, and 54 purse seiners accounted for 31,717 tons of bigeye, 41,406 tons of yellowfin, and 303,127 tons of skipjack. By an order of magnitude, skipjack is the predominant tuna species caught in the Pacific (and elsewhere), but yellowfin catches continue to rise. Most skipjack is canned, but more and more yellowfins are destined for Japanese restaurants, which are on the increase around the world.

Some of the world's most popular food fish are tunas: Yellowfin (top), Albacore (middle), and skipjack (bottom).

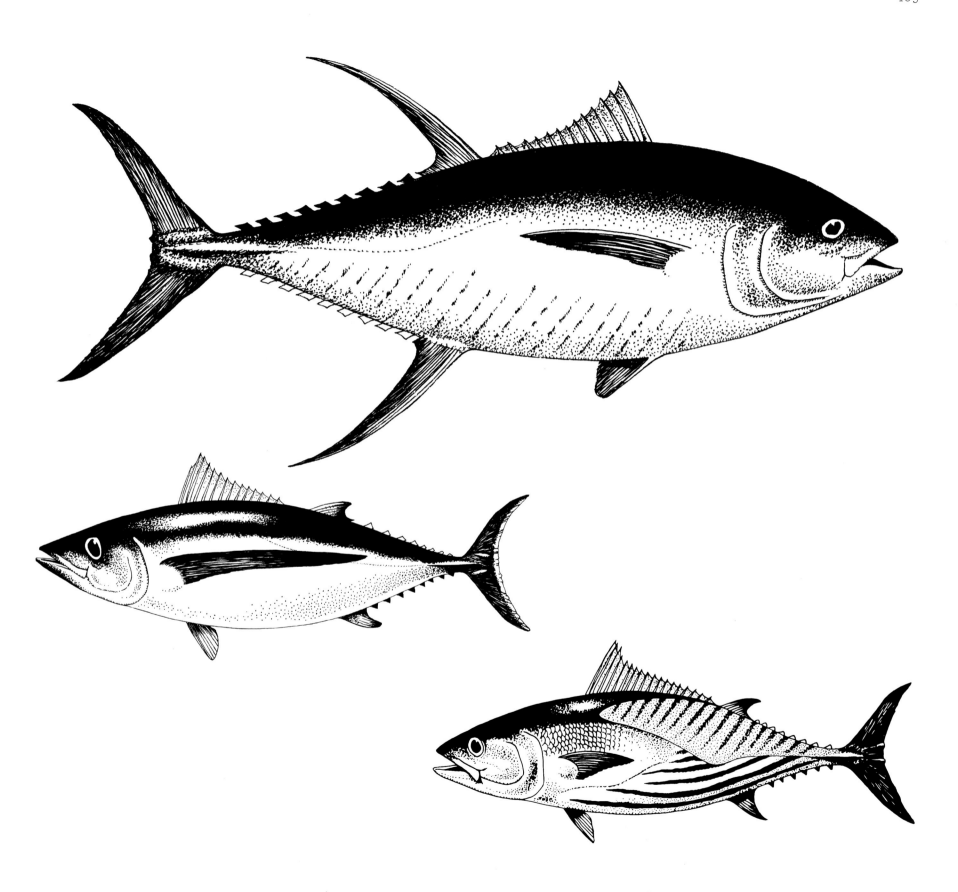

NOT DANGEROUS, BUT BIG

Coelacanth

Giant Sea Bass

Ocean Sunfish

Oarfish

COELACANTH

THE COELACANTH (*Latimeria chalumnae*) is far from the largest fish under consideration here, barely qualifying as a fish that is as big or bigger than a person. The largest known specimen, caught in 1991 off Mozambique, was six feet long and weighed 215 pounds. It is a heavy-bodied, slow-moving fish, with large, patchy scales and fins that seem to be on stalks. It is certainly not as graceful as the billfish nor as dangerous as a shark; when hooked, it comes heavily and reluctantly to the surface. Despite these shortcomings, this ungainly creature is one of the most charismatic of all living fish species. Its importance lies not in its size, beauty, or habitat, but rather in its very existence: Before the first living specimen was found in the twentieth century, it was thought to have gone extinct at the same time as the terrestrial dinosaurs.

On December 23, 1938, fishermen from the South African city of East London hauled in a five-foot-long fish that was steely blue in color, with large bony scales and fins that appeared to be on leglike stalks. Marjorie Courtney-Latimer, a naturalist at the local museum whose specialty was birds, was the first to examine it, and when she could not identify it, she contacted J. L. B. Smith, an amateur ichthyologist and professor of chemistry at Rhodes University in nearby Grahamstown. Smith correctly verified it as a relative of a lobe-finned fish known as *Macropoma*, extinct for about seventy million years. He realized it was a coelacanth, and named it *Latimeria chalumnae* after Latimer and the Chalumna River, near which it was found. Almost fourteen years passed before another was seen, in 1952, but since then many more have been caught, usually in the vicinity of the Comoro Islands between Mozambique and the island of Madagascar. The name *coelacanth*—which means "hollow spines" and refers to its first dorsal fin—was originally used in 1836 to describe the fossil

species. Local fishermen unintentionally catch them, usually while fishing for the oilfish (*Ruvettus pretiosus*). What was once believed to be a stable population of about 650 animals is now thought to number no more than 300, and this rare and zoologically significant creature is probably on the brink of extinction.

The discovery of a living coelacanth has given us an opportunity to peer into the distant geologic past and see a living creature that was previously available only as a fossil. As Keith Thomson wrote in *Living Fossil: The Story of the Coelacanth* (1991): "We cannot take a perch or a cod as a model for understanding its early Devonian ancestors. But *Latimeria* looks very much like the Devonian *Diplocercides* or *Nesides*. Therefore, by studying *Latimeria* in detail, alongside the three lungfishes and in conjunction with the fossils and physical evidence that the rocks themselves provide about the ancient environments in which they lived, we might be able to reconstruct a lot about the biology of these long-distant Devonian forms. And not just the evolution of the skeleton, but the blood, the liver, how they breathed, how they reproduced, how they fed and swam; their whole biology."

In addition to examining collected specimens, biologists have also entered the realm of the free-living coelacanth and filmed it in action, providing a heretofore unavailable view of the life of a Devonian fish. Hans Fricke, a physiologist from the Max Planck Institute in Germany, descended in a submersible off the coast of the Comoros islands in the Indian Ocean, and on January 17, 1987, he became the first human being to film a coelacanth swimming in its natural habitat. Although coelacanths are probably capable of short bursts of speed, they seem to spend most of their time hovering near the bottom with their fins flared. According to Fricke, the extra fin at the tip of the tail is

PREVIOUS SPREAD *The giant sea bass can weigh 600 pounds, but it is not considered dangerous to anything but smaller fishes.*

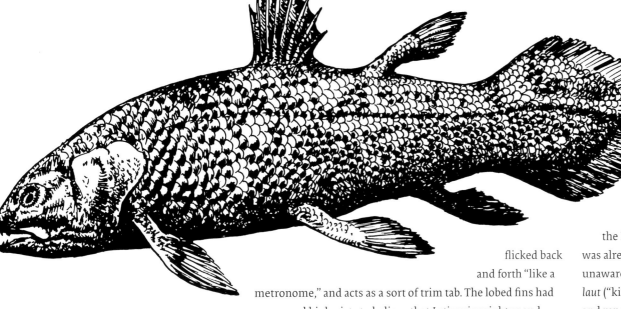

flicked back and forth "like a metronome," and acts as a sort of trim tab. The lobed fins had encouraged biologists to believe that *Latimeria* might spend some time on the bottom, either "walking" or propping itself up on its fins, but Fricke's films only showed that it swam by moving its pectoral and pelvic fins alternately, rather like the walking motions of a tetrapod, such as a dog or a horse. The films were suggestive, but it is not likely that *Latimeria*'s distant ancestors in the sea lent this form of motion to four-legged animals on land, an idea that J. L. B. Smith did little to discourage when he titled his 1956 book on the discovery of the coelacanth *Old Fourlegs*. Even though much of the popular literature places the coelacanth on the list of mammalian ancestors, it is only a distant cousin (female coelacanths give birth to live young and did so long before the arrival of mammals).

Coelacanths spend the day in lava caves and descend to around two thousand feet to forage at night. Comoran fishermen catch them on a hand line, always at night. From his submersible, Fricke has now filmed more than one hundred adult individuals (he has never seen a juvenile), at depths ranging from 385 to 650 feet. They are seen to be passive drift-feeders, opportunistically capturing fish, squid, and octopuses, much in the manner of a large grouper. Fricke also observed a peculiar "head-down" behavior, where the fish spent several minutes at a time in a vertical position with its snout close to the bottom. The coelacanth has an organ at the end of its snout that may prove to be electrically sensitive.

With the exception of the first, all the coelacanths caught prior to 1992 had been found in the vicinity of the Comoros. But in that year, a pregnant female was caught at a depth of about 150 feet off the coast of Mozambique, some eight hundred miles west

of the Comoros. And in 1995 another one was caught off the southeast coast of Madagascar. In 1997, the story changed dramatically. In July of that year, while on their honeymoon, zoologist Mark Erdmann and his new wife, Arnaz Mehta, spotted a coelacanth in a fish market on the tiny island of Manado Tua, off the northern tip of the Indonesian island of Sulawesi. Assuming the coelacanth was already known in the western Pacific, the Erdmanns were unaware of the importance of the fish the Indonesians called *raja laut* ("king of the sea"). When they returned to America, however, and reported what they had seen, they learned of the significance of their sighting and, with funding from the National Geographic Society, went back to Sulawesi the following year, determined to rectify their mistake. For ten months, they scoured the fish markets of northern Sulawesi. They hit pay dirt on July 30, 1998, when they were brought a specimen that was alive, but only barely. (Coincidentally, the Sulawesi coelacanths are caught by fishermen whose target is the same oilfish sought by the Comoran fishermen.) Before they released it, the Erdmanns swam with it and photographed it, hoping it would return to the depths, but it died. Some six thousand miles from East Africa, it appears that there is another, completely unexpected population of coelacanths. In 1999, researchers returned to Manado Tua to look for more Indonesian coelacanths. Although seven dives in the research submersible *JAGO* produced no results, some two hundred miles to the southwest, in the region of Kuandang, they found two specimens living in deep caves at a depth of five hundred feet. Whereas the Comoran coelacanths inhabit lava caves on young volcanic slopes, those off Sulawesi live near much older, less steep, and more eroded formations, with very few caves. Moreover, the waters of north Sulawesi are subject to much stronger currents (estimated peak velocity of three or four knots) than the regions where the Comoran coelacanths have been observed, suggesting a different lifestyle for the two species. "The biogeography of the new coelacanth population remains enigmatic," wrote Fricke and colleagues (one of whom was Mark Erdmann), "although perhaps this is for the best. An undiscovered home is probably the best possible protection for these endangered fish."

GIANT SEA BASS

Fishermen sometimes try to catch these giants, but instead of fighting, the fish hunkers down in or under rock formations, making the angler feel as if he is trying to reel in a small locomotive. The giant sea bass feed on crustaceans and fish, which they inhale into their capacious mouths. These mouths are probably capable of swallowing a smallish human, and there are many reports of giant bass emerging ominously from their rock hideaways to investigate divers, but no reports of sea bass "attacks" have ever been authenticated.

THROUGHOUT THE WORLD'S WARMER, inshore waters, there are several gigantic bass that are variously called sea bass or groupers. The giant sea bass (*Stereolepis gigas*) is the California version, prowling the coastal bottoms of the Pacific. The record for this blotchy, greenish brown fish, caught in 1968 off Anacapa Island, is 563 pounds. It has been estimated that a fish of this size might have been seventy-five years old. The goliath grouper (*Epinephalus itajara*) is another giant sea bass, found in the western Atlantic from Florida to Brazil (including the Gulf of Mexico) and in the eastern Pacific from Costa Rica to Peru. It frequents regions no more than sixty feet deep, although it occasionally wanders into deeper waters. It can be differentiated from the giant sea bass because it has more soft rays than spines in the dorsal fin and a rounded tail fin (the giant sea bass has a tail that is concave on its terminal margin). The IGFA-record goliath grouper weighed 680 pounds and was caught in Florida in 1961.

The Indo-Pacific giant sea bass is the Queensland groper (*Protomicrops lanceolatus*), one of the largest of all reef fish. It is known to achieve a weight of 880 pounds and may grow even larger. The common and scientific nomenclature of this fish is completely muddled; it is sometimes referred to the genus *Epinephalus*, and throughout its range, it is called brindle bass, garrupa, goliath grouper, and giant grouper. All of these species are also known as "jewfish," a name thought to be derived from anti-Semitic characterizations of a form that many find ugly, but it is being dropped from current usage.

OPPOSITE *Throughout the world's warm inshore waters, there are different versions of the giant sea bass. Under slightly varied names, these monsters are found off California, Florida, and Queensland, Australia.*

RIGHT *Considerably larger than the man who caught it, this giant sea bass, caught off Catalina Island, California, weighed 428 pounds.*

If weight is the criterion, the ocean sunfish is the largest of all bony fishes, weighing in at two tons or more.

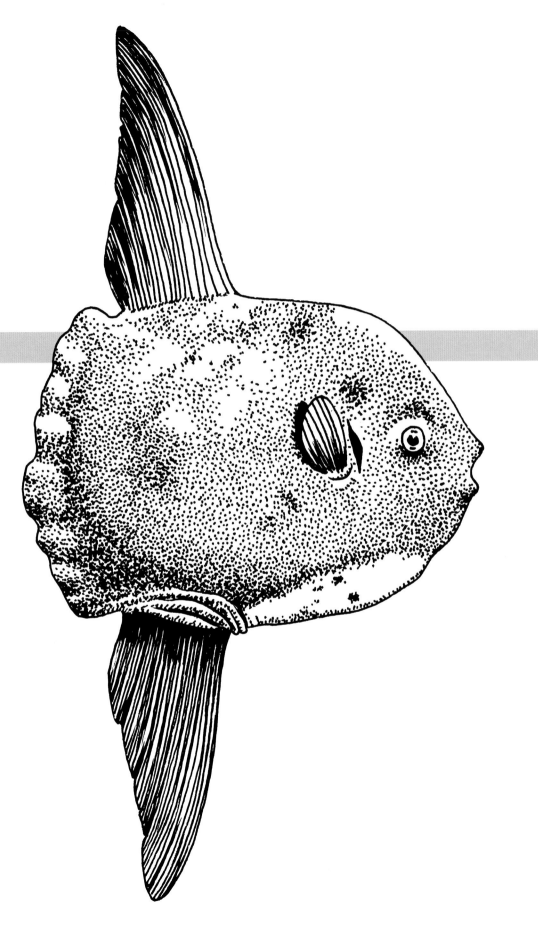

OCEAN SUNFISH

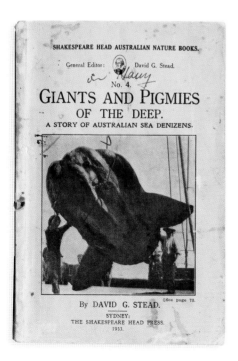

IN THE WORLD outside the ocean, the largest animal is easy to identify. The largest living land animal is the African elephant; in Angola in 1974, E. M. Nielsen, an American big-game hunter, shot a bull that measured thirteen feet eight inches at the shoulder, and whose weight was estimated at twelve tons. As far as we know, the blue whale, at a length of one hundred feet and a weight of three hundred thousand pounds, is the longest and heaviest animal that has ever lived on earth. But what criteria shall we use to identify the largest fish? The whale shark and the basking shark are cartilaginous fish, so they are placed in a different category than the bony fish. For the osteichthyes, if length is the criterion, the flimsy oarfish, at a known length of twenty-six feet, is probably the record holder. (There are stories of oarfish fifty feet in length, but these are usually found on the "sea serpent" shelves of the library.) Swordfish, marlins, and bluefin tuna have been caught at weights approaching a ton, and big-game anglers like to eulogize these graceful and powerful predators as the largest of their kind, but if weight is the criterion, the billfish and tuna must be relegated to the second rank. The heaviest bony fish ever weighed is the decidedly unlovely ocean sunfish, also known as *Mola mola*. Mola means "millstone" in Latin, and there is probably not a more appropriate description for this creature.

A huge relative of the triggerfish and puffers, the ocean sunfish is the heaviest of all the bony fish. With its terminally placed dorsal and anal fins and its almost nonexistent tail, it appears to be all head. Molas feed largely on jellyfish, a diet in which volume must make up for its low nutritional value. It was once thought that they spend most of their time floating at or near the surface as though dead, but recent research suggests that Molas are deep divers and it is possible that their basking behavior on their sides in the sun is for the purpose of restoring body heat after time spent at depth.

How heavy is the ocean sunfish? On September 18, 1908, off Bird Island, forty miles out of Sydney, the SS *Fiona* was subjected to an enormous concussion and brought to a complete standstill. Examination revealed a gigantic carcass entangled in the port propeller, and because the crew was unable to remove it, the *Fiona* chugged into Sydney Harbor with the carcass attached. An iron hook was specially wrought to lift the carcass from the water, and it was discovered to be a gigantic slab of a fish, later identified as an ocean sunfish. Ichthyologist David Stead, who was present when the great fish was lifted from the water, used its photograph as the cover illustration for his book, *Giants and Pigmies of the Deep.* He wrote that its weight was, "estimated by the Captain and the winchman of the *Fiona* to be about 2 tons. Its length was 10 feet 2 inches, greatest depth across the dorsal and anal fins 13 feet 4 inches, thickness 2 feet 6 inches." Somehow, the estimated weight of "about 2 tons" became 4,928 pounds—an increase of almost half a ton—in Gerald Wood's *Guinness Book of Animal Facts and Feats*, but that is well within the range of those who tell the stories of very large fish.

OARFISH

EVEN THOUGH THEY HAVE RARELY been seen alive—and even more rarely by people who know what they are seeing—the ribbon fish or oarfish (*Regalecus glesne*), sometimes called "king of the herrings," may be responsible for some of the most dramatic sea-serpent stories. Known to reach a length of twenty-six feet, the oarfish is a laterally flattened creature with a coral red "cockscomb" of spines on its head and a red dorsal fin that runs the length of its body. It is so poorly known that few ichthyologists would venture to guess at its habits, but an oarfish swimming at the surface with its crest erect could easily bring the classical image of a sea serpent to mind.

The oarfish has a silvery, ribbonlike body, a pair of long, slender pelvic fins with flattened tips (the "oars" of its common name), and a scarlet, cockscomblike crest (part of the dorsal fin) that it can erect above its head. It is probably the longest bony fish in the world, but there are no documented records of specimens longer than twenty-six feet. Joseph Nelson's *Fishes of the World* (1984) and Margaret Smith and Phillip Heemstra's *Sea Fishes* (1986)—two of the most reliable general works on fish—give 26.5 feet as the maximum known length. At this length, an oarfish would probably weigh less than a thousand pounds, demonstrating the difficulty in identifying the world's largest bony fish. (The heaviest is the ocean sunfish, which has been weighed at almost five thousand pounds. The largest fish of any kind, of course, is the whale shark, which can reach a length of fifty feet, and weigh more than ten tons.)

No one but a trained ichthyologist would recognize an oarfish at the surface, so if we assume that this creature sometimes pokes its head out of the water while swimming, we might be able to account for some serpent sightings. It would not make a very formidable sea serpent, since it is a fragile, almost transparent creature that is totally harmless. But because of its spectacular appearance on the beach (and occasional appearance in the water) several authorities have firmly affiliated it with sea-serpent stories. In *The History of Fishes* (1963), Norman writes that "the Sea Serpents of Aristotle, Pliny, and other classical authors

seem to have been nothing more than gigantic eels. The monster described as having the head of a horse with a flaming red mane is the Oarfish or Ribbonfish, a species which probably grows to more than fifty feet in length, and may sometimes be seen swimming with undulating movements at the surface of the sea." In his *In the Wake of the Sea Serpents*, Bernard Heuvelmans tells of a naval officer in 1860 who sent a letter from Bermuda to the British journal *The Zoologist*, in which he said that he had found "a strange sea monster... the animal being no less than the great sea serpent." He then went on in great detail to describe an oarfish.

With the rare exception of an occasional oarfish that washes ashore and can be examined, virtually nothing is known of its biology. (When examined, their stomachs have been found to contain the tiny, shrimplike euphausiids known as krill—the predominant food of some baleen whales.) A videotape shot from the Japanese submersible *Shinkai-6500* in 1998 contains what is probably the first underwater footage of a live oarfish. It is swimming almost at the surface. In July 1996, a dive-boat operator named Greg Willis was snorkeling in the Sea of Cortez when he noticed "a long dark figure" approaching him. His first thought was "shark," but then he noticed a strange red crest and a long thin body "slanting way down into the water" (the quotes are taken from an article in the *Los Angeles Times*, dated August 7, 1996). When Willis dived with the oarfish—for that is exactly what it was—he saw that part of its tail was missing, seemingly bitten off by some animal, perhaps a shark. Willis swam right up to the fish and saw "an eye, a large, saucer-shaped eye with a black pupil, set into a huge silver face crested by long, lucent red fins that the fish arched higher as I approached from behind." He grabbed the fish and went for a little ride, but the fish shook him off and headed for shallow water, where it thrashed around and died. Willis and his mates hauled it up on the beach and measured it at eighteen feet six inches. It was then cut up into pieces and taken to the University of Baja California Sur at La Paz. Photographs confirm its identification and size.

OPPOSITE *The oarfish, sometimes known as the ribbon fish, is the longest bony fish in the world. It has been measured at twenty-six feet in length, but there are unsubstantiated reports of much longer ones.*

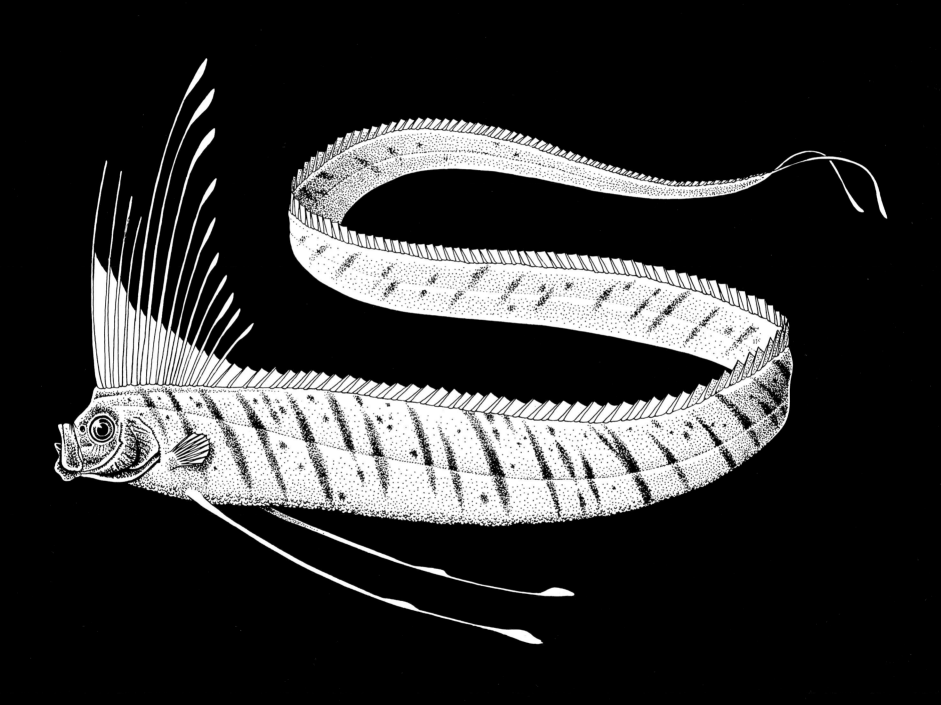

GIANTS OF LAKES & RIVERS

Chinese Paddlefish

Sturgeon

Arapaima

Alligator Gar

Wels

Giant Mekong Catfish

CHINESE PADDLEFISH

IN CHINESE IT IS KNOWN AS *pinyin* or *báixún*. Its scientific name is *Psephurus gladius*. *Psephurus* is from the Greek *psephas*, "dark," and *oura*, "tail." *Gladius* means "sword," and although the paddle is distinctly unswordlike, the paddlefish shares this specific name with the bearer of the most effective weapon in the fish world, the broadbill swordfish, *Xiphias gladius.*

What do we know about *Psephurus gladius?* For one thing, we are not really sure how big it gets (or, rather, got—it is currently believed to be extinct). There are anecdotes about twenty-one-footers, but these seem to have been estimated, not measured. There is a tale about one that was twenty-three feet long, but this is unconfirmed by anything that might be considered evidence. From old photographs, *Psephurus* appears to have been a larger version of the American paddlefish, *Polyodon spathula*, and as befits a creature of murky rivers, it is a nondescript gray above and lighter below. If the Chinese paddlefish can only be distinguished from its American counterpart by size and geography (not to mention the former's nonexistence), we might assume that it shares some of its smaller relative's habits. As with many other plankton eaters, paddlefish swim through aggregations of tiny creatures, trapping them in their gill rakers. From specimens observed in captivity, we know that the American paddlefish do not use the "paddle" for rooting in the bottom, but rather as a sensory organ for detecting swarms of plankton in the roiled and cloudy waters in which they live. Secondarily, they use it as a sort of guide to direct food into the capacious mouth. But unlike, say, the basking shark, which simply opens its mouth and swims through plankton, the paddlefish

distorts its entire head to increase the capacity of its open mouth. "Watching the feeding through the glass," wrote Earl Herald, longtime director of the Steinhart Aquarium in San Francisco, "the visitor is astonished when the paddlefish opens its mouth. The entire back part of the head drops down, and one gets the feeling that he is watching something anatomically impossible." (In the definitive *Fishes of the World*, Joseph Nelson writes that *Polyodon* has a "non-protrusible mouth," while *Psephurus* has a "protrusible mouth," suggesting that the Chinese paddlefish could, in addition to dropping its lower jaw, extend its mouth parts forward.)

The Chinese (or, more specifically, the Yangtze) paddlefish was so poorly known that its passing was hardly noticed. Tucked into a 2006 news story about the probable extinction of the Chinese river dolphin (*Lipotes vexillifer*) titled "A Fellow Mammal Leaves the Planet" was this line: "In addition to *baiji* [the Chinese name for the dolphin] the Yangtze paddlefish is (was) the largest freshwater fish in the world (at least 21 feet), and it hasn't been seen since 2003; the huge Yangtze sturgeon breeds only in tanks now because it has no natural habitat (a huge dam stands between it and its breeding grounds)." In the Yangtze, habitat modification, pollution, and heavy boat traffic may have turned the Chinese paddlefish into "the living dead," says ecologist David Dudgeon of the University of Hong Kong, in the sense that individuals may possibly survive but the species is doomed.

Paddlefish, extinct and extant, although counted among the bony fish, or osteichthyes, have mostly cartilaginous skeletons, which places them in a very special category, which includes such big fish as sturgeons and gars, as well as some smaller,

The Chinese paddlefish, one of the largest freshwater fish in the world, is now extinct.

and relatively primitive, species such as bichirs and the bowfin. Sharks, the marine vertebrates that are the living exemplars of cartilaginousness, are not, as is commonly assumed, more "primitive" than the bony fish; the earliest osteichthyes predate the earliest known sharks by millions of years, and paddlefish fossils have been found that predate the dinosaurs by fifty million years. The term "living fossil" is essentially oxymoronic, as fossils are defined as remnants of extinct forms and therefore cannot be alive, but its meaning is clear. Charles Darwin first introduced the concept of a "living fossil" in *The Origin of Species* (1859). He wrote, "As we here and there see a thin straggling branch springing from a fork low down on the tree, and which by some chance has been

favoured and is still alive at its summit, so we occasionally see an animal like *Ornithorhynchus* [the platypus] or *Lepidosiren* [the lungfish], which in some small degree connects by its affinities two large branches of life, and which has apparently been saved from fatal competition by having inhabited a protected station." How could some creatures make it through the mass extinctions, climatic anomalies, swooping temperature variations, the wobbling of the earth on its axis, extraterrestrial bombardments, and other perturbations that wiped out nearly everything else? We may never know the answer to this broad question, but it is clear that all protected stations in nature become vulnerable eventually, and *Psephurus gladius* has lost its safe harbor.

STURGEON

STURGEON ARE ANCIENT, CARTILAGINOUS fish from a family more than sixty million years old. Even if they were not characterized as "living fossils," the sturgeons look like holdovers from another era. They are heavy fish whose bodies are covered with five rows of scutes, or plates, that run from the gill covers to the base of the tail. Their gill covers also consist of huge, bony plates, and their heads are covered with smaller bony plates. Their skeleton is mostly cartilage. They have an upturned snout and threadlike barbels, whiskerlike organs that are situated before a protrusible, tubelike mouth. In all sturgeons (as in all sharks and paddlefish), the upper lobe of the tail is longer than the lower.

Most sturgeon species are anadromous (that is, they live in coastal waters and ascend streams and rivers to breed), but there are some species that are landlocked, spending their entire lives in lakes or rivers. They are bottom-feeders, consuming insect larvae, small fish, and, occasionally, fish-related carrion. In rivers that support salmon populations, sturgeon will forage on salmon roe as well as on decaying salmon remains.

Sturgeon are also among the largest of the bony fish; the record is said to be a twenty-four-foot-long beluga sturgeon (*Huso huso*) that was caught in the Volga River in 1827 and weighed 3,249 pounds. Today, beluga specimens of ten to twelve feet are considered large. The white sturgeon (*Acipenser transmontanus*) is the largest freshwater fish in North America, once found in river systems from Alaska as far south as central California and known to reach a weight of 1,800 pounds. Though legally protected since 1921, this sturgeon has never really recovered from its past exploitation, due primarily to its long reproductive cycle. In large river systems such as the Fraser River in southern British Columbia and Oregon's Columbia River, however, white sturgeon in excess of fifteen feet and weighing more than 1,500 pounds can still be found, and life spans of one hundred years are not unusual.

In the 1800s, sturgeon often became entangled in commercial fishing nets, and the fish were discarded as a worthless nuisance. Today, the sturgeon is recognized as one of the world's most important commercial fish, prized especially for its caviar. Although the meat is edible and popular in some parts of Europe, sturgeons are best known for their eggs. A single female can lay upwards of three million eggs in each spawning cycle, and it is these tiny black spherules that have led to the downfall of sturgeon populations around the world. Beluga caviar is made from the most famous eggs in the world, comparable in mythic and monetary value to the golden eggs of a certain goose. Of course, that goose would keep laying golden eggs as long as it was not killed, but to get the eggs from a sturgeon, you have to kill it. If you kill the spawning females they will never spawn again, and if you eat the eggs, they will never grow up into more sturgeons. That is the reason sturgeons are endangered.

Beluga caviar is a somewhat curious appellation, at least in the English translation, because beluga means "white" in Russian—as in the eponymous whale—and beluga caviar is black. The Russian sturgeon (*Acipenser gueldenstaedti*) is another species found in the Black, Azov, and Caspian seas, as well as the rivers entering into them. This fish produces osetra caviar, light gray to brownish or golden yellow in color, and with a nutty flavor. Some caviar connoisseurs feel that it is the best tasting of all caviars. The sevruga sturgeon (*Acipenser stellatus*) produces sevruga caviar, having the smallest grains of all, a light gray to dark gray/black color, and a very buttery, somewhat smooth flavor. All other sturgeon lay eggs in vast quantities, and eggs from other species are harvested as a delicacy, but historically these three species from Russia are the source of the most highly valued caviar.

In an extensive 1993 study, Vadim Birstein of the Russian Academy of Sciences identified no fewer than twenty-one species of sturgeon, most of which are considered endangered, vulnerable, rare, or extinct. In North America, five of the nine species of sturgeon—along with the closely related paddlefish—are listed as endangered, while in the Caspian Sea, which historically has been home to the world's largest abundance of sturgeon, annual catches have dropped by 95 percent in the past hundred years, from more than twenty thousand tons in the early 1900s to only one thousand tons in the late 1990s. Many government and international agencies have tried to regulate sturgeon fisheries, particularly in Russia, but the high price of caviar continues to draw poachers and black-market smugglers into an illegal trade.

When faced with a catastrophic decrease in one of the world's most economically important food items, humans—who had been directly responsible for the decrease in the first place—found a way to keep the supply of caviar flowing: They began to breed sturgeons in captivity. Because the price of caviar will always remain high (the highest-grade beluga caviar now sells for more than $100 an ounce, and prime-grade osetra and sevruga caviar retails for around $60 and $44 an ounce, respectively),

sturgeon farming is an attractive prospect—over time. Belugas normally take thirty years to go from fry to egg-laying age in their natural environment. Without natural enemies—particularly sturgeon fishermen, who typically kill females for their eggs—the sturgeons can mature and lay eggs much faster.

There is a beluga "farm" in Florida and several in California. Almost every European country has established sturgeon-raising facilities, including Italy, France, Spain, Germany, and Poland. Not to be outdone, countries along the Caspian Sea, such as Iran, Russia, Turkmenistan, and Kazakhstan, where sturgeons have been fished almost to extinction, are building the requisite tanks and stocking them with sturgeons. Sturgeon farming is not rocket science: You capture some immature sturgeons, put them in artificial ponds, feed them, and wait for them to breed and lay eggs. By carefully monitoring and regulating water temperature (the sturgeon's growth and reproductive processes are accelerated in warmer water), as well as providing a high quality diet, sturgeons can be encouraged to spawn in seven to nine years instead of the twenty or thirty required in the wild. Scientists have also discovered that injecting the females with hormones spurs the development of eggs, and there are even experiments in hybridization under way. As a result of the rise of sturgeon farming, we have saved some species from extinction; it is amazing how quickly people can act when there is money to be made.

The sturgeon is endangered in the wild because the eggs of the female, which has to be killed in the process, are packaged as caviar. Sturgeon farming guarantees that some species will not disappear.

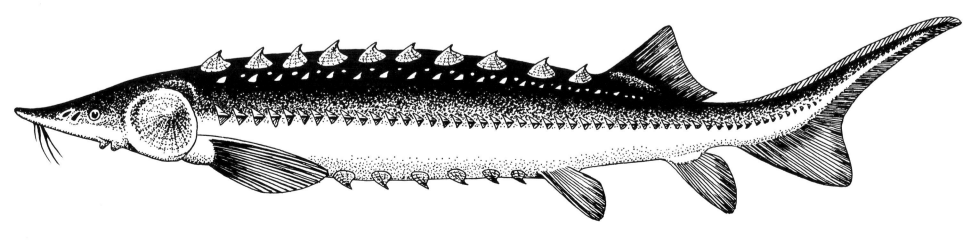

ARAPAIMA

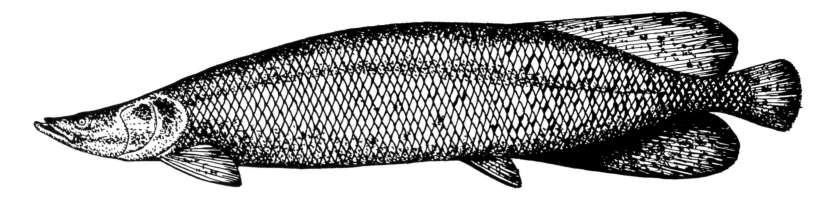

IN HIS *GUINNESS BOOK OF ANIMAL Facts and Feats*, Gerald Wood begins his discussion of the arapaima (*Arapaima gigas*) with this statement: "Some writers claim that the largest freshwater fish in the world is the arapaima, also called the pirarucu, which is found in the Amazon drainage of Ecuador, Peru, and Brazil, but the size attained by this fish has been greatly exaggerated." While there are reports of arapaima reaching fifteen feet in length and weighing one thousand pounds, most of the larger specimens that have been reliably measured did not exceed eight feet in length and weighed no more than four hundred pounds. Still, a four-hundred-pound fish lurking in the Amazon River is a pretty big fish, and one that is more than a little likely to engender the kind of exaggeration that we call "fish stories," such as, "you should have seen the one that got away."

A rather primitive-looking fish, with large scales, a low-slung prognathous mein, and fins placed far back on its body, the arapaima is slow moving. Because its air bladder is richly supplied with blood vessels and serves as a sort of lung, the arapaima is an obligate air breather and therefore has to surface for a breath every fifteen minutes or so. Being an air breather is an advantage in the oxygen-poor waters of the Amazon, and even allows the arapaima to survive periods of drought by burrowing in swampy mud. Unfortunately for the arapaima, however, being a slow fish that surfaces frequently makes it an easy catch for humans with harpoons on the shore or in canoes. Arapaima have been known to eat birds, but more to the point, humans like to eat arapaima, with consequent pressure on the species.

Because of its size, the arapaima is a popular exhibit in public aquariums, as is its smaller relative, the arawana (*Osteoglossum bicirrhosum*). In *Living Fishes of the World* (1961), Earl Herald, former director of the Steinhart Aquarium in San Francisco, described it fondly: "In spite of its being a large, heavy-bodied fish, it moves with a smooth and sinuous grace, which explains why aquarists prize it so highly…. It has large, olive-green scales, and the posterior part of the body… is increasingly reddish toward the tail until at the caudal peduncle it becomes crimson." Herald noted also its rapid growth: "One specimen grew from 8 to 64 inches in five years."

In addition to being a local food fish (and a source for nail files made from its scales), the arapaima is a popular target for sportfishermen in South America, but it is not recognized as a game fish by the IGFA. (Curiously, the arawana, a much smaller fish, is; the all-tackle record is ten pounds twelve ounces.) Around 1972, thirty-five arapaimas from the Amazon were airlifted to Thailand and introduced into Bung Sam Lan Lake, an artificial, private lake created from a swamp. Along with the gigantic Mekong River catfish, the arapaima has become one of the magnets that draw anglers to the jungle rivers and lakes of Southeast Asia. They hope, as almost all anglers do, to be able to brag about catching a really big fish.

Introducing South American arapaimas into an artificial Thai lake raises a question of authenticity, as well as the ethical one of "shooting fish in a barrel." If the fish have been introduced from a river system to a lake, does catching one really qualify as "sport-fishing"? Even more important, if the fish are in an environment unlike their original one, where there are different prey species—and no natural predators—how can a real record be claimed? One might as well fish in an aquarium, where the fish does not have to chase down its food, but is fed regularly, getting fatter and fatter, and therefore that much more susceptible to attaining "world-record" size.

ALLIGATOR GAR

It looks like a fish with an alligator's head grafted on, but the alligator gar is all fish. The world record is 365 pounds.

THE NAME "GAR," LIKELY DERIVED FROM the *Old English* word for "spear," was originally used for a species of North Atlantic needlefish (*Belone belone*), and later extended to the family of fish known as Lepisosteidae. Gars are primitive, ray-finned fish that come in various sizes, but are all long, slender creatures with pincerlike jaws. Their heavy scales are diamond-shaped and interlocking, and do not overlap as do the scales of most other fish. These so-called ganoid scales were used in jewelry making by Indians; "gar scale jewelry" is still found in the American South today. Unlike other gars, the alligator gar (*Atractosteus spatula*) possesses a double row of large teeth in the upper jaw, which is obviously responsible for the front half of its common name. It is also unique among gars in that it is capable of breathing air: An alligator gar can survive for up to two hours out of the water.

The alligator gar is the largest species of gar and the largest exclusively freshwater fish in North America, native to rivers and lakes in the southeastern United States. The IFGA rod-and-reel world-record alligator gar was seven feet nine inches long and weighed 279 pounds. It was caught in the Rio Grande River in Texas in 1951. Even larger alligator gars have been caught by trotlines: These are usually made with rope or cord bearing numerous baited hooks. The unofficial record belongs to Kirk Kirkland of Texas, who caught a 365-pound specimen almost ten feet long in 1991. This aggressive, solitary fish lives on a diet of fish but occasionally catches waterfowl and has, in some rare cases, been known to bite humans (almost certainly because it mistakes a foot or hand trailing in the water for a fish). It has even been witnessed attacking a five-foot alligator before devouring it.

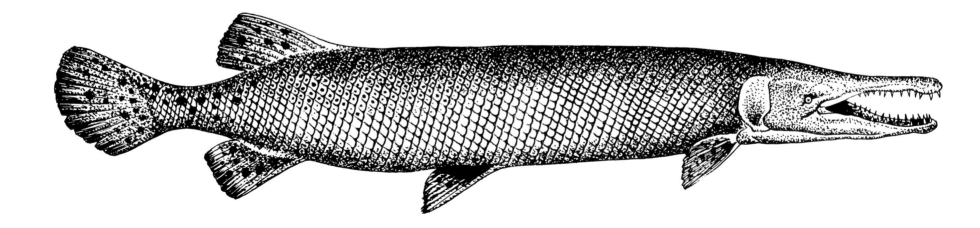

WELS

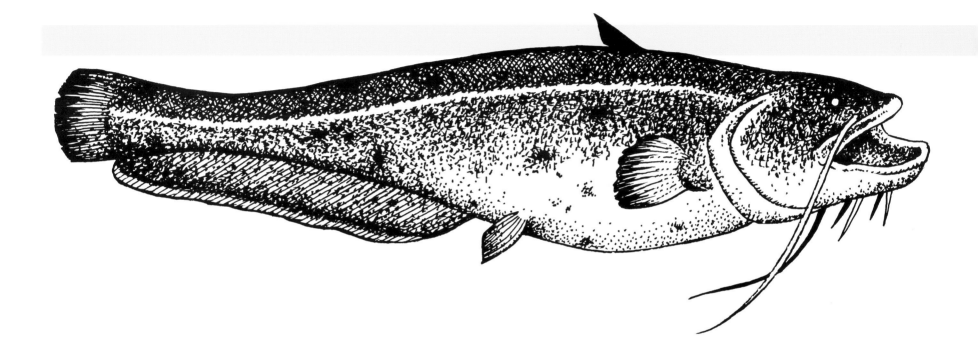

The giant European catfish known as "wels" has long sensitive feelers that enable it to find food in silty, cloudy rivers.

ANOTHER MEGA-CATFISH IS THE WELS (*Silurus glanis*), found throughout the lakes and rivers of central and eastern Europe ("wels" is the German name for this fish). A bottom-feeder, its scaleless body is graced by a long anal fin and a face whose wide mouth sports three pairs of barbels—one pair on the upper jaw and two on the lower. It feeds on fish, frogs, and crayfish, and is said to be particularly fond of eels. Its size and wide mouth probably contributed to its reputation as a man- or child-eater, but such stories seem to fade under close inspection.

The IGFA lists this species as a game fish, but posts no records. There is, however, no shortage of records to be found in the literature, ranging from generalizations such as, "the wels... is said to exceed 12 feet in length and weigh hundreds of pounds"

(Edward Migdalski and George Fichter, 1976, *The Fresh and Salt Water Fishes of the World*), to Gerald Wood's very specific account of the "largest accurately measured wels of which there is reliable evidence was a 9 foot 10 inch female caught in the Danube in Rumania [and] the heaviest Russian fish that was taken in 1918 in the Desna River in the Ukraine that weighed 565 pounds." Wood wrote that, "before it was overfished, the European catfish was considered the largest freshwater fish in the world," but it is unlikely that it ever approached the heft of the giant Mekong catfish. The largest reliably reported wels was an Italian specimen, caught in the Po River, that measured 9 feet 1.5 inches and weighed 317 pounds.

GIANT MEKONG CATFISH

At a weight of more than 600 pounds, the giant Mekong river catfish is a desirable game fish, but it is being overfished.

THE LOWER MEKONG RIVER, which forms the border of Laos and Thailand, and crosses Cambodia before reaching the sea in Vietnam, is home to the giant Mekong catfish, *Pangasianodon gigas*, probably the world's biggest freshwater fish (given that sturgeon are anadromous), reaching up to ten feet in length and in excess of six hundred pounds in weight in a life span of approximately sixty years. In a 2004 article, Zeb Hogan, probably the foremost authority on this giant, said it "grows as fast as a bull and looks a bit like a refrigerator." Its scaleless, muscular body is silvery bronze on the back, lighter on the prominent belly; its head is wide and flat, with a lipless, toothless mouth; and its eyes are set so low—often on a line with or slightly below the mouth—that photographs of this species often look as if they have been published upside down. Unlike other catfish species, the Mekong giant has no whiskers. From October to December each year, the species migrates from Tonlé Sap, a huge lake on a tributary of the Mekong in Cambodia, into the mainstream of the river. From there, it is believed to move upstream to spawn.

This giant catfish, which has been feeding villages on the Mekong for as long as the bluefin tuna in the Mediterranean, is now one of the most endangered fish in Southeast Asia. It is still found in the Tonlé Sap and at Ramsar in northeastern Cambodia, although neither of these sites yet offers true protection for the species. In Cambodia, it is illegal to capture, sell, or transport the giant Mekong catfish, but "bagnet" fishers ignore the law. The situation is the same in Thailand, where tourists and the media are attracted to fishing sites in spite of conservation laws. Alongside overfishing, the main threats to the species include habitat loss, dams that block migration, and genetic intermingling with cultured stocks. The fish was bred in captivity for the first time in 2001, but individuals artificially spawned

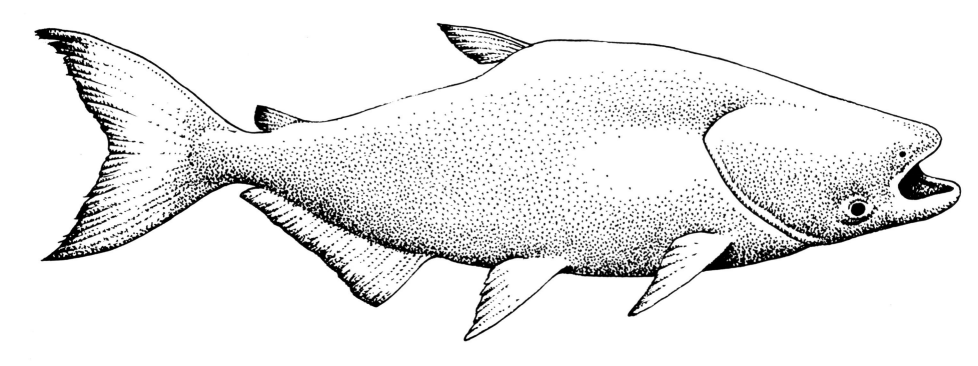

A Mekong River catfish is much larger and heavier than the fishermen who caught it.

from wild-caught parents have been released into the Mekong since 1985. Few of them survive to reach their full size any more, but fishermen caught one in May 2005 that was nine feet long and weighed 646 pounds, now considered the record for a freshwater fish of any species.

The giant catfish fulfills all the traditional criteria for a game fish: It is certainly big enough, and according to Jean-François Helias, who runs Fishing Adventures Thailand in Bangkok, it is "widely accepted as being the hardest fighting freshwater fish on the planet… it makes fast, determined takes, followed by unstoppable runs… this fish will test the angler and his tackle to the limit every time." That is, if the angler can find one.

The plight of the giant catfish highlights the need for precautionary actions to aid in species conservation, including increased effort to understand the ecology and status of

imperiled fish before they disappear. Quoted in *Science* in 2007, environmental scientist Thomas Lovejoy said of the giant Mekong catfish, "These are iconic fish. Much like tigers on land, they are the flagship species representing the wonders of life in the rivers."

WHAT IS THE FATE OF THE BIG FISH?

ALTHOUGH MOST FISH THAT PEOPLE EAT are small enough to be manageable in nets—salmon, cod, mackerel, pollack, herring, sardines, anchovies, and so forth—there are some very large species that appear regularly on menus. Indeed, swordfish and tuna, among the largest of all bony fish, are also among the world's favorite food items. There is only one kind of swordfish, but there are many kinds of tuna that do not qualify as giants, such as skipjack, albacore, and yellowfin. The bluefin, the ne plus ultra of tuna, reaches a weight of 1,500 pounds—and because of one country's insatiable lust for its raw flesh, it is being hunted almost out of existence. Once known as "horse mackerel," the bluefin was considered so undesirable that it was fed to cats and dogs; from that lowly position, over a period of not more than half a century, it has become the most valuable fish in the world. In 2001, a single bluefin was sold at the Tsukiji fish market in Tokyo for $173,000.

The future of the bluefin tuna is written in Japanese. It is more than a little painful to realize that *Thunnus thynnus*, the most highly evolved fish in the world, is literally being eaten out of existence. Bluefin tuna have the misfortune to be on or near the top of the list of "most desirable food fish." At the dock and in restaurants, prices for these fish rise as their numbers diminish. This sounds like nothing more than a traditional "supply and demand" equation, but the difference between fishing for wild species and manufacturing is that once the fish are gone, you cannot make any more.

The fate of the bluefin is not an anomaly—it is the norm. Almost all of the large pelagic species—swordfish, marlins, sharks—are in trouble, and the cause is invariably overfishing. More than one hundred million sharks per year are killed in the macabre process known as finning, but this is not the sole cause of the destruction of shark populations. It was a novel that so altered the world's perceptions of sharks that people all around the world began killing them, claiming, of all things, "self-defense." The novel, of course, was Peter Benchley's *Jaws*, which was published in 1974 and was made into the first modern blockbuster movie the following year. "Just when you thought it was safe to go back in the water" read the ads, and the putative reason it was unsafe was that the water was filled with man-eating sharks. So to make the water safe, people tried to kill all the sharks. For more than thirty years, the *Jaws* mentality—"the only good shark is a dead shark"—has goverened our attitude toward sharks. Even today, few people mourn the plight of the oceanic whitetip, once one of the most numerous of large sharks and now considered endangered.

Only the truly weird fish, with no food value and posing no

Off Sandy Hook, New Jersey, in 1964, fisheries biologists hauled in ten juvenile white sharks on a single longline.

threat to humans, have been spared the onslaught. We have no idea about the numbers of the oarfish, as it is only rarely seen, and the ocean sunfish, observed occasionally basking at the surface, is widely reputed to be inedible (and therefore safe from fishermen). The Chinese paddlefish will never again be bothered by fishermen—it is extinct.

Analyzing the data from Japanese longliners over the past fifty years and combining that with U.S. and Australian scientific/ observer data for the same period, Boris Worm and Ransom

Myers of Dalhousie University, along with Marcel Sandow, Andreas Oschlies, and Heike Lotze of Germany's Leibniz Institute for Marine Science, documented the extent of the loss. Their data, published in *Science* in July 2005, showed that oceangoing longliners were catching half the number of fish—and half the number of species—that they were able to catch in the 1950s. To no one's surprise, overfishing was found to be the major cause of the decline, but temperature anomalies such as El Niño also contributed, as did habitat destruction and climate change. The reduction in species diversity—primarily the removal of the large predators such as tuna, swordfish, and cod—leaves an ocean ecosystem vulnerable to environmental changes such as global warming. Worm, interviewed by Cornelia Dean of *The New York Times*, observed that the world's tuna fishery today is largely yellowfin and skipjack, because bluefin and albacore rarely appear on fishermen's lines. Said Worm, "If the ocean changes in a way that doesn't favor these two species [yellowfin and skipjack] any more, we have very little to fall back on. If you have a rich diversity of species, it's like a diverse stock portfolio."

It was always assumed—at least by fishermen—that as a particular fish species grew scarce, the fishermen would simply find another place to fish. Or if a particular species declined, the fishermen would find another species. There are, after all, a lot of fish in the sea. But this rosy attitude has proved to be disastrously flawed. If you take most of the population of a given species of fish out of the ocean, there may not be enough left to perpetuate the species. When Myers and Worm looked into the worldwide historical fisheries records, they found that over the past half century, populations of the large predatory fish—cod,

Commercial fishermen are depleting the stocks on which they fish. Here Sicilian fishermen pull in a swordfish.

tuna, marlins, swordfish, sharks, and rays—had plummeted by 90 percent. In other words, only 10 percent of these popular food fish have survived what Carl Safina has called "scorched-earth fishing."

Populations of marine creatures that are not food fish have been shown to be in steep decline during the same period: Sea turtles, whales, dolphins, seals, sea lions, and sea otters have been hunted, fished, clubbed, or shot so that, in many cases, their populations are now regarded as endangered. Raking the bottom in pursuit of groundfish like cod, haddock, pollock, redfish, and grenadiers, trawlers have been mowing down the fragile corals like bulldozers. In her 1999 testimony before congress on the subject of endangered oceans, marine scientist Sylvia Earle likened this method of fishing to dragging nets through marshes to capture ducks and geese, bulldozing forests to take songbirds, or dynamiting trees to catch squirrels. In a 2000 letter to *The New York Times*, ichthyologist Elliot Norse made clear just how huge the damaged area was: "On an annual basis, trawlers scour an area equivalent to twice the size of the lower 48 states.... An activity that each year disturbs an area of seabed as large as Brazil, the Congo, and India combined must affect the structure, species composition, and biogeochemistry on both local and global scales."

Fisheries biologist Daniel Pauly of the University of British Columbia is the author of the phrase "fishing down the food chain." Fishermen take the apex predators first (large species such as cod, tuna, and swordfish), because they are the most desirable species. After these are gone, they go down a trophic level and take the apex predators' prey species (plankton eaters such as anchovies). And then they take what is left. (From the Greek *trophe* meaning "food" or "nourishment," a "trophic level" refers to the ranking of prey species eaten by a particular group of fish.) "Fishing down the food chain" means trading a limousine for a bicycle. This downward shift has already occurred. To gauge the extent of the loss of species, researchers have assigned numbers to each trophic level (although the distinctions are not as clear as one would like them to be because many creatures feed from multiple levels). Putting aside the predators at the very top of the chain, *Homo sapiens*, apex hunters such as tuna and swordfish are level 4.0; level 3.0 is given to the prey of these predators—squid, anchovies, and the like; level 2.0 is reserved for the zooplankton, such as copepods, on which creatures at level 3.0 feed; and at the bottom, 1.0, are the phytoplankton that support the whole

There are still giant tuna in New England waters. This 920-pounder was caught from Captain Gary Cannell's Tuna Hunter *out of Gloucester, Massachusetts.*

structure. Pauly, working with Villy Christensen, Rainer Froese, and Maria Lourdes Palomares, was able to calculate the overall global trophic level of fish catches over time. "We firmly believe," they wrote in a 2000 *American Scientist* article, "that the trophic level... is truly declining."

The paradigm for this disaster was the wholesale removal of the codfish, one of North Atlantic's top predators and once the dominant species of the Scotian Shelf, which extends from the coast of Nova Scotia to the edge of the continental slope, which have been reduced to such low levels that the American and Canadian cod fisheries have been shut down. Just as the removal of wolves from some areas in North America had a "top-down," ripple effect on the entire ecosystem, so too did the removal of the cod in the North Atlantic affect every trophic level, starting a cascade that rumbled down the food chain through the smaller

fish that they fed on, from the newly dominant crab and shrimp, all the way down to the plankton and algae. This major shift on the Scotian Shelf means, among other things, that the cod stocks may never recover. In their 2005 review of the effects of removing the cod from the system, Kenneth Frank and his colleagues concluded: "The changes in top-predator abundance and the cascading effects on lower trophic levels... reflect a major perturbance of the eastern Scotia Shelf ecosystem.... One must acknowledge the ecological risks inherent in 'fishing down the food web,' as is currently occurring on the Scotian Shelf, or the ramifications associated with indirect effects reverberating across levels throughout the food web, such as altered primary production and nutrient cycling."

"Fishing down the food chain," of course, is not restricted to human fishers, but the concept helps one understand the ramifications of overfishing by humans. In Monterey Bay, California, first the sea otters were hunted to near extinction, which meant that the sea urchins on which they fed could proliferate unchecked. The urchins in turn gnawed on the holdfasts that anchored giant kelp, which was thereby cut loose to float on the surface, thus eliminating the entire habitat of the fish that called these great kelp forests home. Writing in 2003 on worldwide fish populations, Daniel Pauly and Reg Watson declared "overfishing has slashed stocks—especially of large predator species—to an all-time low worldwide, according to new data. If we don't manage this resource, we will be left with a diet of jellyfish sandwiches and plankton stew." The rampant destruction of fish populations has resulted in an ecological crisis of unprecedented proportions. Because our lives are so tied to the sea, our very future depends on how we resolve this crisis.

Aristotle and his contemporaries had no way of estimating the population size of fish that they were describing, but it is not unreasonable to assume that they thought the numbers were infinite. In 1961, Hawthorne Daniel and Francis Minot published *The Inexhaustible Sea*, a book described on the jacket as, "The exciting story of the sea and its endless resources." Daniel and Minot had not been reading the newspapers carefully, because as they were writing their book, journalists were reporting that the anchovy population off the coast of Peru was crashing. Anchovies (genus *Engraulis*) and sardines (genera *Sardina* and *Sardinops*) are among the most important of all commercially fished species. The California sardine fishery celebrated by John Steinbeck in his 1945 novel *Cannery Row* had its peak catch of 1.5 billion pounds in 1936, but almost ceased to exist by 1962. The *anchovetas* from the Peru Current existed in such vast numbers that they once headed the list of largest commercial catches: More than eleven million metric tons were caught in 1967. But this fishery collapsed in 1973 (due not just to overfishing, but also to the El Niño of that year), and the *anchoveta*, once considered one of the most numerous fish in the world, is now classified as an endangered species.

During the past millennia, we have learned much about the ocean and its inhabitants. To the ancient Romans, the Mediterranean, which they knew as *Mare Nostrum* ("our ocean"), was inhabited by an assortment of fish and shellfish that constituted the known extent of marine life. From bacteria to whales, we now recognize some 210,000 species of living things in the ocean, and the number is on the increase. Much of the information we have gathered is new—that is, it was unknown a generation ago. Then, we did not know that hot vents bubbled from the ocean floor, that sea cucumbers swam far from the bottom, or that coelacanths had set up shop in Indonesian waters. Through the window of population modeling, we can now see the Caribbean as Columbus did, teeming with thirty million green turtles rather than the million left today.

Because it encompasses what we know and, to a certain extent, what we recognize we do not know, we tend to think of scientific investigation as a process that has brought us to the present state of knowledge. But combining the known and the unknown leads inexorably to the unknowable; we cannot predict what devices or methods will be invented to enable us to better understand the nature of life in the marine environment. Steadily evolving scientific methodology has revealed some disturbing realities: Marine fish species, whales, and shellfish populations are down around the world, often beyond levels of possible recovery. Will new technologies enable us to find new populations or new species to fish? Probably not; there is only so much that technology can do.

Contrary to widespread popular belief, fishing is a far greater threat to marine life than "pollution." It stands to reason, after all, that killing large numbers of fish is going to have more of an effect on the population of a given species than dumping garbage or even oil. But, as Pauly, Watson, and Jackie Alder, his colleagues at the University of British Columbia, argue in a 2005 article in the *Philosophical Transactions of the Royal Society*, people did not seem to understand this simple equation, and they say that the reason "has to do with notions from another age, when fishing was indeed a matter of wrestling one's sustenance from a foreign, hostile sea, and from tiny boats, close to one's village, using equipment barely capable of making a dent in the huge populations of fish known to inhabit the ocean's unfathomable depths." That image, they suspect, is still prevalent, even though the commercial fisheries industry is now a giant enterprise that "is having so severe an impact on its own resources base that, if present trends continue, it will collapse in the next decades, and drag down with it, into oblivion, many of the fishes it exploits, together with their supporting ecosystems."

Man's "dominion" over the animals of the land and sea has

The Tsukiji fishmarket in Tokyo, where of thousands of tons of bluefins are auctioned off daily, destined for sushi and sashimi restaurants.

proved to be an almost unmitigated disaster. Some years ago, at a meeting of the International Whaling Commission, I asked Sylvia Earle, then deputy commissioner of the U.S. delegation, why she thought the whalers appeared so eager to destroy the resource upon which their industry depended. She answered: "Think of oil, timber, coal, and any number of fishes, birds, and mammals. Whenever humans have had the opportunity to exploit a natural resource, they have overexploited it." So it is

with the big fish. Industrial-strength overfishing has reduced many open-ocean species to skeletal numbers. Sportfishing for giants (for which read: world records) has proved irresistible to man the hunter. The freshwater giants have been systematically deprived of the very waters they inhabit, as we drain the lakes, dam the rivers, and poison the very waters themselves. Being a big fish, then, is the equivalent of receiving an engraved invitation to the extinction party.

Sources

Anderson, P. S. L., and M. W. Westneat. 2007. Feeding mechanisms and bite force modeling of the skull of *Dunkleosteus terrelli*, an ancient apex predator. *Biology Letters* 3, 76–79.

Bandini, R. 1933. Swordfishing. *California Fish and Game*. 19:241–248.

—. 1939. *Veiled Horizons: Stories of Big Game Fish of the Sea*. New York: Derrydale Press.

Baughman, J. L. 1948. Sharks, sawfishes, and rays: their folklore. *American Midland Naturalist* 39(2):373–381.

—. 1955. The oviparity of the whale shark *Rhincodon typus*, with records of this and other fishes in Texas water. *Copeia* 1 (3) 112–123.

Baum, J. K., and Myers, R. A. 2004. Shifting baselines and the decline of pelagic sharks in the Gulf of Mexico. *Ecology Letters* 7(2):135–11.

Baum, J. K., R. A. Myers, D. G. Kehler, B. Worm, S. J. Harley, and P. A. Doherty. 2003. Collapse and conservation of shark populations in the northwest Atlantic. *Science* 299:389–392.

Benchley, P. 1974. *Jaws*. New York: Doubleday.

—. 1982. *The Girl of the Sea of Cortez*. New York: Doubleday.

—. 1998. Swimming with sharks. *Audubon* 100(3):52–57.

—. 2000. Great white sharks. *National Geographic* 197(4):2–29.

—. 2002. *Shark Trouble*. New York: Random House.

Benton, M. 1977. *Vertebrate Paleontology*. London: Chapman and Hall.

Bigelow, H. B., and W. C. Schroeder. 1948. *Fishes of the Western North Atlantic, Part 1: Sharks*. New Haven, CT: Sears Foundation for Marine Research.

Birstein, V. J. 1993. Sturgeons and paddlefishes: threatened fishes in need of conservation. *Conservation Biology* 7(4):773–787.

Budker, P. 1971. *The Life of Sharks (La Vie des Requins)*. New York: Columbia University Press. (Orig. French edition, Paris, 1946.)

Buel, J. W. 1887. *Sea and Land: An Illustrated History of the Wonderful and Curious Things of Nature Existing Before and Since the Deluge. A Natural History of the Sea, Land Creatures, the Cannibals, and Wild Races of the World*. New York: Lewis Historical Publishing Co.

Carey, F. G. 1973. Fish with warm bodies. *Scientific American* 228(2):36–44.

Carey, F. G., and J. M. Teal. 1966. Heat conservation in tuna fish muscle. *Proc Natl Acad Sci* 56(5):1464–69.

Compagno, L. J. V. 1984. *Sharks of the World. FAO Species Catalog. Vol. 4. Part 1: Hexanchiformes to Lamniformes*. Rome: U.N. Development Programme.

—. 1984. *Sharks of the World. FAO Species Catalog. Vol. 4. Part 2: Car-charhiniformes*. Rome: U.N. Development Programme.

Compagno, L., M. Dando, and S. Fowler. 2005. *Sharks of the World*. Princeton, NJ: Princeton University Press.

Coppleson, V. M. 1958. *Shark Attack*. Sydney: Angus & Robertson.

Cousteau, J.-Y. and P. Cousteau. 1970. *The Shark: Splendid Savage of the Sea*. New York: Doubleday.

Cousteau, J.-Y. and F. Dumas. 1963. *The Silent World*. New York: Harper & Row.

Daniel, H., and F. Minot. 1961. *The Inexhaustible Sea*. New York: Collier Books.

Darwin, C. 1859. *The Origin of Species by Means of Natural Selection*. London: John Murray.

Davies, D. H. 1964a. The Miocene shark fauna of the southern St. Lucia area. *Oceanographic Research Institute Investigational Report* 10:1–16.

—. 1964. *About Sharks and Shark Attack*. Pietermaritzburg, South Africa: Shuter & Shooter.

Dean, B. 1909. The giant of ancient sharks. *Amer. Mus. Jour.* 9(8):232–34.

Dewhurst, W. H. 1835. *The Natural History of the Order Cetacea and the Oceanic Inhabitants of the Arctic Regions*. London.

Earle, S. A. 1995. *Sea Change: A Message of the Oceans*. New York: Fawcett Columbine.

Ellis, R. 1975. *The Book of Sharks*. New York: Grosset & Dunlap.

—. 2003. *The Empty Ocean*. Washington, DC: Island Press.

—. 2008. *Tuna: A Love Story*. New York: Knopf.

Ellis, R., and J. E. McCosker. 1991. *Great White Shark*. Palo Alto, CA: Stanford University Press.

Erdmann, M. V. 1998. Sulawesi coelacanths. *Ocean Realm*. Winter 1998–99:26–28.

Erdmann, M. V., R. L. Caldwell, and M. K. Moosa. 1998. Indonesian "king of the sea" discovered. *Nature* 395:335.

Erdmann, M. V., R. L. Caldwell, S. L. Jewett, and A. Tjakrawidjaja. 1999. The second recorded living coelacanth from north Sulawesi. *Environmental Biology of Fishes* 54:445–451.

Farrington, S. K. 1949. *Fishing the Atlantic, Offshore and On*. New York: Coward-McCann.

—. 1953. *Fishing the Pacific, Offshore and On*. New York: Coward-McCann.

—. 1971. *Fishing with Hemingway and Glassell*. New York: McKay Press.

Fitch, J. E., and R. J. Lavenberg. 1971. *Marine Food and Game Fishes of California*. Berkeley, CA: University of California Press.

Fricke, H. W., and K. Hissmann. 1991. Coelacanths–the fate of a famous fish. *Oceanus* 34(3): 44–45.

Fricke, H., K. Hissmann, J. Schauer, M. Erdmann, M. K. Moosa, and R. Plante. 2000. Bio-geography of Indonesian coelacanths. *Nature* 403:38–39.

Garrick, J. A. F. and L. P. Shultz. 1963. A guide to the kinds of potentially dangerous sharks. pp. 3–60 in P. Gilbert, ed., *Sharks and Survival*, Washington, DC: D.C. Heath.

Gilbert, P. W., and C. Gilbert. 1973. Sharks and shark deterrents. *Underwater Journal* 5(2):69–79.

Goadby, P. 1972. *Big Fish and Blue Water*. Holt, Rinehart and Winston.

Gore, M., D. Rowat, J. Hall, F. R. Gell, and R. F. Ormond. 2008. Transatlantic migration and deep mid-ocean diving by basking shark. *Biology Letters* doi:10.1098/rsbl.2008.0147.

Grey, Z. 1919. *Tales of Fishes*. New York: Harper & Brothers (1990 Edition, Derrydale Press).

—. 1925. *Tales of Fishing Virgin Seas*. New York: Harper & Brothers.

—. 1927. *Tales of Swordfish and Tuna*. New York: Harper & Brothers.

—. 1931. *Tales of Tahitian Waters*. New York: Harper & Brothers (1990 Edition, Derrydale Press).

—. 1934. The great mako. *Natural History* 34(3): 8–13

Gudger, E. W. 1915. Natural history of the whale shark. *Zoologica* 1(19):8–20.

—. 1940. The alleged pugnacity of the swordfish and the spearfishes as shown by their attacks on vessels. *Journal of the Asiatic Society of Bengal* 12(2):215–315.

—. 1941. The food and feeding habits of the whale shark, *Rhineodon typus*. *Journal Elisha Mitchell Science Society* 57(1):1–14.

Heilner, V. C. 1953. *Salt Water Fishing*. New York: Knopf.

Hemingway, E. 1952. *The Old Man and the Sea*. New York: Scribner's.

—. 1970. *Islands in the Stream*. New York: Scribner's.

Herald, E. S. 1961. *Living Fishes of the World*. New York: Doubleday.

Hogan, Z. S., P. B. Moyle, B. P. May, J.Vander Zanden, and I. G. Baird. 2004. The imperiled giants of the Mekong. *American Scientist* 92:12–20.

Housby, T. 1982. *The Rubby-Dubby Trail: Shark Fishing in British Waters*. London: Gentry Books.

Heuvelmans, B. 1965. *In the Wake of Sea Serpents*. New York: Hill & Wang.

Isaacs, J. P. and R. A. Schwarzlose. 1975. Active animals of the deep sea floor. *Scientific American* 233(4):84–91.

IUCN. 2006. *2006 IUCN Red List of Threatened Species*. www.iucnredlist.org. Downloaded on 19 June 2007.

Joseph, J., W. Klawe, and P. Murphy. 1988. *Tuna and Billfish: Fish Without a Country.* La Jolla, CA: Inter-American Tropical Tuna Commission.

LaGorce, J. O. 1952 (ed.). *The Book of Fishes.* National Geographic Society.

LaMonte, F. 1952. *Marine Game Fishes of the World.* New York: Doubleday.

——. 1958. *North American Game Fishes.* New York: Doubleday

——. 1965. *Giant Fishes of the Open Sea.* New York: Holt, Rinehart and Winston.

Lineaweaver, T. H., and R. H. Backus. 1973. *The Natural History of Sharks.* New York: Anchor Doubleday.

Maggio, T. 2001. *Mattanza: The Ancient Sicilian Ritual of Bluefin Tuna Fishing.* New York: Penguin.

Martill, D. M., and J. D. Hudson. 1991. *Fossils of the Oxford Clay.* London: The Palaeontological Association.

Martill, D. M., E. Frey, R. P. Caceres, and G. C. Diaz. 1999. The giant pachycormid *Leedsichthys* (Actinopterygii) in the Southern Hemisphere: further evidence for a Jurassic Atlanto-Pacific marine faunal province. *N. Jb. Geol. Paläont. Mh* 1999:243–256.

Mather, C. O. 1976. *Billfish: Marlin, Broadbill, Sailfish.* Auckland: Saltaire.

Matthiessen, P. 1971. *Blue Meridian: The Search for the Great White Shark.* New York: Random House.

Maxwell, G. 1952. *Harpoon Venture.* New York: Viking.

Melville, H. 1851. *Moby-Dick.* New York.

Migdalski, E. C. 1958. *Angler's Guide to the Salt Water Game Fishes, Atlantic and Pacific.* New York: Ronald Press.

Migdalski, E. C., and G. S. Fichter. 1976. *The Fresh and Salt Water Fishes of the World.* New York: Knopf.

Mitchell Hedges, F. A. 1923. *Battles with Giant Fish.* London: Duckworth.

Mundus, F., and B. Wisner. 1971. *Sportfishing for Sharks.* New York: Macmillan.

Myers, R. A., and B. Worm. 2003. Rapid worldwide depletion of predatory fish communities. *Nature* 423:280–83.

Nakamura, I. 1985. *Billfishes of the World.* (FAO Species Catalog). *FAO Fisheries Synopsis* 125(5). Rome.

Nichols, J. T., and F. R. LaMonte. 1935. The Tahitian black marlin, or silver marlin swordfish. *Amer. Mus. Novitates* 807:1–2.

——. 1937. Notes on swordfish at Cape Breton, Nova Scotia. *Amer. Mus. Novitates* 901:1–7.

Norman, J. R., and F. C. Fraser. 1938. *Giant Fishes, Whales and Dolphins.* New York: W. W. Norton.

Norman, J. R., and P. H. Greenwood. 1963. *A History of Fishes.* New York: Hill and Wang.

Pauly, D., and R. Watson. 2003. Counting the last fish. *Scientific American* 289(1):42–47.

Pauly, D., V. Christensen, R. Froese, and M. L. Palomares. 2000. Fishing down aquatic food webs. *American Scientist* 88(1):46–51.

Pauly, D., V. Christensen, J. Dalsgaard, R. Froese, and F. Torres. 1998. Fishing down marine food webs. *Science* 279:860–63.

Raloff, J. 2007. Hammered saws. *Science News* 172(6):90–92.

Randall, J. E. 1963. Dangerous sharks of the Western Atlantic. pp. 39–61 in P. Gilbert, ed., *Sharks and Survival.* Washington, DC: D.C. Heath.

Randall, J. E. 1973. The size of the great white shark (*Carcharodon*). *Science* 181: 196–70.

Safina, C. 1995. The world's imperiled fish. *Scientific American* 273(5):46–53

——. 1997. *Song for the Blue Ocean.* New York: Henry Holt.

——. 1998a. Song for the swordfish. *Audubon* 100(3):58–69.

——. 1998b. Scorched-earth fishing. *Issues Sci. Technol.* 14(3):33–36.

Scott, W. B., and S. N. Tibbo. 1968. Food and feeding habits of the swordfish, *Xiphias gladius*, in the Western North Atlantic. *Jour. Fish. Res. Bd. Canada* 25(5):903–19.

Simões, P. R. and J. P. Andrade. 2000. Feeding dynamics of swordfish (Xiphias gladias) in Azores area. *Col. Vol. Sci. Pap. ICCAT* 51(5): 1642–46.

Smith, J. L. B. 1950. *The Sea Fishes of Southern Africa.* Cape Town, South Africa: Central News Agency, Ltd.

——. 1956. *Old Fourlegs: The Story of the Coelacanth.* London: Longmans Green & Co.

——. 1933. *Giants and Pygmies of the Deep: The Story of Australian Sea Denizens.* Sydney, Australia: The Shakespeare Head Press.

——. 1963. *The Sharks and Rays of Australia.* Sydney, Australia: Angus & Robertson.

Steinbeck, J. 1945. *Cannery Row.* New York: Viking.

Steinberg, J. 2002. It's a mola. *National Geographic* 202(5):64–68.

Taylor, L. R., L. J. V. Compagno, and P. J. Struhsaker. 1983. Megamout—a new species, genus, and family of lamnoid shark (*Megachasma pelagios*, family Megachasmidae) from the Hawaiian Islands. *Proc. Cal. Acad. Sci.* 43(8):87–110.

Thomson, K. S. 1991. *Living Fossil: The Story of the Coelacanth.* New York: W. W. Norton.

Tinsley, J. B. 1964. *The Sailfish: Swashbuckler of the Open Seas.* Gainesville, FL: University of Florida Press.

Travis, W. 1961. *Shark for Sale.* Rand McNally.

Walters, V., and H. Fierstine. 1964. Measurements of swimming speeds of yellowfin tuna and wahoo. *Nature* 202:208–209.

Ward, P., and S. Elscot. 2000. *Broadbill Swordfish: Status of World Fisheries.* Canberra, Australia: Bureau of Rural Sciences.

Worm, B., M. Sandow, A. Oschlies, H. K. Lotze, and R. S. Myers. 2005. Global patterns of predator diversity in the open ocean. *Science* 309:1365–1369.

Wood, G. L. 1982. *The Guinness Book of Animal Facts and Feats.* Enfield, England: Guinness Book .

Zarudzki, E. F. K. 1967. Swordfish rams the 'Alvin.' *Oceanus* 13(4):14–18

INDEX

Page numbers in italics refer to illustrations.

ACKNOWLEDGMENTS

At its largest, the ocean sunfish, also known as Mola mola, *is the heaviest of all bony fish, weighing in at more than two tons.*

FILLED AS IT IS with paintings, photographs, drawings, anecdotes, personal obserations, and references, it is obvious that many people had to have contributed to this book. I did the paintings and drawings, but in many cases, somebody else photographed them. Art photographer Bob Mates is responsible for many of the professional-looking photographs; I took the photographs that are not so brilliant. My first-hand experiences with big fish probably began when I lived in Rhode Island and had the opportunity to work with shark biologists Jack Casey, Chuck Stillwell, and Wes Pratt, of the National Marine Fisheries Service Laboratory in Narragansett. I've had personal encounters with many kinds of big fish, and even some fossil fishes (in museums), but to identify every person who was with me or assisted me over the years would take more space than is available, so I will simply list those people who contributed to my knowledge and experience: James Atz, Barbara Block, Jack Casey, Genie Clark, Harry Fierstine, Rodney Fox, Gordon Hubbell, Marie Levine, John McCosker, Ransom Myers, Pat Smith, Rob Staunton, Leighton Taylor, Ron and Valerie Taylor, Wes Pratt, Carl Safina, Tierney Thys, and Kiwi White. My friends Peter Gimbel, Perry Gilbert, and Peter Benchley are gone, but I am indebted to them for their encouragement in my pursuit of information, and in some cases, pursuit of the fish themselves.

Sydney Shuman, who is the diver shown in the painting of the whale shark, provided a transparency of the painting when I couldn't find one; Gail Morchower, librarian of the International Game Fish Association helped enormously with photographs of big game fish and their captors; Karen Canell sent me (and appears in) the photograph of the giant tuna caught off Gloucester, Massachusetts; Jean-Francois Helias, of Fishing Adventures Thailand, allowed me to use his photo of the arapaima (that's him in the middle); those are Matthew Potensky's wonderful photographs of a living hammerhead and a whale shark with a diver; Mark Ferrari generously allowed me to reproduce the photograph of the swordfish that stabbed him; the Greenland shark in the St. Lawrence was photographed by Chris Harvey-Clark; the mola by Mike Johnson; and Tonya Wiley supplied the historic photo of captured sawfish.

This book, and everything in it, is for Stephanie.

Editor: Eric Himmel, with Eric Klopfer
Designer: Neil Egan
Art Director: Michelle Ishay-Cohen
Production Manager: Alison Gervais

Library of Congress Cataloging-in-Publication Data

Ellis, Richard, 1938–
 Big fish / by Richard Ellis.
   p. cm.
 ISBN 978-0-8109-9626-7 (harry n. abrams, inc.)
 1. Marine fishes. 2. Fishes —Size. I. Title.

 QL620.E45 2009
 597.022′2—dc22

                           2008042779

Printed and bound in China
10 9 8 7 6 5 4 3 2 1

HNA ▮▯▮▮▯
harry n. abrams, inc.
a subsidiary of La Martinière Groupe
115 West 18th Street
New York, NY 10011
www.hnabooks.com